MIDST OF HIS BROTHERS

TIM SMITH

Midst of His Brothers

Edited by Brian Hunter @
www.anoitedwritenow.com

Cover Design by Cynthia D. Johnson @
www.diverseskillscenter.com

Printed in the United States of America

Website: http://www.blessingheights.org

ISBN-13: 978-1495440083

Table of Contents

Introduction... 5

Acknowledgments 10

The King Anointer.................................... 13
Among the Stuff.......................................45
Fill Your Horn Again.................................63

Midst of His Brothers.................................81

Keeper of Sheep or Searcher of Mules..................97

Bigger They Are the Harder They Fall.................121

The One with the Anointing 139

Royal Robe 157

Eyes of Saul 183

As King...201

Epilogue...224
Glossary...229
About the Author.................................237

Introduction

The book of I Samuel has always been a favorite reading of mine. The lives of Samuel, Saul, and David reveal such a powerful history which began the monarchy of the Jewish nation of Israel.

My desire is, in retrospect, to both compare and contrast the lives of these men with the operation of leadership in the church world today. They are unique in many ways and are also similar to each other.

Samuel, who had a heart for Israel, was searching out a king to lead those who would fully obey the voice of the Lord while also praying that Israel would prosper and grow in power and strength. His faithfulness to the Lord and dedication to God's people are likened to none other.

He truly was a faithful servant.

Saul, with strong leadership abilities but weakness in faith and self-confidence, started off well. However, in time his insecurities began to surface. Instead of working with God, he ended up fighting against the Almighty's desire for His people.

David was a man after God's own heart. He did not begin with much wealth or great strength, but he possessed faith with which to overcome any situation he faced. With the exception of Jesus Christ, David's leadership surpassed all others ever to lead Israel before or since.

Others mentioned include Jonathan, David's brothers, and Abner, all of whom had great impact on the kings and kingdoms of Israel.

In I Samuel, God's Word is more than just a story or history of the Jewish nation. It is an insight to the operations of the spiritual world and how the forces of light and darkness operate in the battle for the church and the nations.

There is a great struggle in the heavens to establish God's holy people here on the earth, to set in order the right government that will lead them to victory over their adversaries. God will always have a people who will stand and represent His name here on earth.

My desire is to show some of the things I believe are taking place in the church world today. There are some who are called to be Samuel's, to stand up and call out the David's in the crowd that God has chosen for this next generation and move of His Spirit. There are also Saul's out there who are in the body of Christ but have become disconnected from obeying the voice of God and are now unwittingly hindering the plan that God is implementing for this generation.

I hope this book will challenge you for the sake of your ministry. When you are called, only you can accomplish the work that has been placed before you. No one else can fulfill your God called destiny.

This book will most likely be different than other books you may have read. I don't consider myself an author. I never even had the desire to write a book until recently. However, I believe it was the Lord who started dealing with my heart and leading me to write these thoughts concerning I Samuel.

If you are in ministry now or prayerfully considering going into ministry, I hope that this book will give you some direction concerning God's way of dealing with His people and those He has called into leadership.

Acknowledgments

First and foremost, highest praise and deepest thanks to my Lord and Savior Jesus Christ who is and always will be my best and closest friend. Appreciation and love to the lovely lady God has gracefully joined to my heart and soul through holy matrimony, Diana, and to the two best children a dad could ever hope for, Angel and Clay. Love and gratitude to my godly parents who raised my siblings and I in a Spirit filled home, Robert and Bonnie Smith. And, much love, appreciation, and encouragement to the great congregation of folks at Blessing Heights Church who have allowed me to be their pastor and shepherd for the past eighteen years. Thanks also to Brian Hunter, my editor and friend, who has helped me so much with this first book.

MIDST OF HIS BROTHERS

Chapter One
The king anointer.

Abraham Lincoln, the sixteenth president of the United States, is considered by many to be the greatest president in American history. His accomplishments and abilities held the country together while critical, necessary changes he made exhibited great leadership. He also endured countless personal struggles such as the loss of his own son while making key decisions for his country. Abraham Lincoln was a great president and a great man. But, who made him great?

Undoubtedly, much of his greatness must be attributed to him. However, there was one to whom he also contributed much of his success, his stepmother, Sally Bush, of whom Lincoln said, "God bless my mother. All that I am or ever hope to be I owe to her." (Basler, 1969, p. 108) Sally Bush was indeed a very intelligent woman who exhibited practical good sense. She was neat and caring while teaching Abraham how to dress, read, write, and be all that he could be. In one of Abraham Lincoln's statements as president, he referred to her as his angel because of her doting love and affection. He referred to himself the son whom she rescued from squalor, ignorance, and degradation to ultimately become a much honored statesman.

Great makes great

Sally Bush was never president and, in fact, not a lot of people today have even heard of her. She merely prepared a young boy to be one of the greatest presidents America would ever know. It takes a great person to make a great person.

Like Sally Bush-Lincoln, the prophet Samuel was one of those great people God used to make others great. Hannah, his mother, was barren. She made a promise to God that, if He would give her a son, she would give him back to the Lord. From the moment of

Samuel's conception, Gods hand was at work in his life. When he was born, Hannah kept him until he was weaned, took him to the temple of the Lord, and left him there. She did not break her vow even though a son was what she had desired more than anything. And so, Samuel was brought up under the guidance of Eli, the High Priest, and trained in the godly ways of the priesthood. God communed with Samuel even at an early age. His behavior and demeanor were noticed among the Israelites.

When Eli the priest died and the Philistines took the Ark of the Covenant, the people quickly turned to Samuel for direction. He stepped into this leadership role without hesitation. Israel had lost a crucial battle to their enemy and the nation's most sacred possession, the Ark of the Covenant, was gone. Without the Ark, they felt they were cut off from hearing God's voice and would be unable to win any future battles against the Philistines. The Ark, where the mercy seat rested as its lid, was the instrument which housed the powerful presence of God. This was the place where the High Priest would meet with the Lord to hear His voice.

During that period of time, when Eli was High Priest and judge he placed his two sons, Hophni and Phinehas, into position as priests over the daily sacrifice. They were unfaithful to the service of the Lord, taking advantage of the people and all that was brought to be sacrificed unto the Lord. This caused the people of Israel to lose trust in the priests and the temple. Then they also feared for their lives and despaired of losing the Ark. The nation's confidence in the priesthood was shaken.

That was the situation in Israel when Samuel became a judge. It was a chaotic time with the land in despair and in great need of solid godly leadership. Many wondered if Samuel or anyone else could ever restore Israel to a higher place, restoring honor, trust, and security.

We read nothing of any great capabilities that Samuel possessed such as supernatural strength like Samson or great wisdom like Solomon. Nor did Samuel possess considerable wealth. However, he was a man that believed and honored the Lord in all of his ways. The Bible makes a statement about Samuel's integrity, stating that none of his words fell to the ground. Everything he said came to pass. All of Israel knew this of him and many would travel from afar just to seek his counsel for their own lives.

Samuel was Israel's spiritual coach

With Samuel's guidance and leadership, Israel stayed intact. Even though, under his leadership, Israel did not wipe out the Philistines nor broaden its borders, they kept from falling into despair and defeat. Samuel taught them the good Word of the Lord. He sowed good seeds into their minds and hearts. His godly discretion and instruction brought them back to a place of worshiping and obeying the Lord God of Israel.

When I was a freshman in high school, I was on the basketball team in Marissa, IL. Our team was called the Meteors. We were not a spectacular team, but I did learn a many fundamentals from our coach. Unfortunately, I did not do anything with those fundamentals except improve my street ball skills. When I joined the team I could barely chew gum and dribble the ball at the same time. Coach was working hard to get us ready not just to play ball, but to win. He made us go over the same plays again and again until we knew them by heart.

Samuel was Israel's spiritual coach. He set out to help Israel live successfully in the land that God had given them. At my home town of Marissa, IL, this was our basketball coach's first year. He was told that our team "the Meteors" would most likely not win a single game all year. Our team was at the bottom of the barrel and he set out to teach us the basic principles of basketball. We had a lot of show offs, but no real team skills. The first thing he did was sit all the glory seekers down and promote team strategies. At first this did not go over well.

Some of the guys felt they were too good to sit on the bench, so they quit the team. This farm boy was just happy to be on a real high school basketball team. We all realized that we were going to have to do it coach's way which meant we would have to work together. Things started clicking pretty well after that. We ended up winning a game toward the end of the season. Compared to what we looked like to begin with, you could tell we had greatly improved and learned to follow instructions.

His heart was connected to the will of God

Samuel was stepping into a position where the people not only needed instructions, but they had been left with a warped vision of true and proper obedience to God by Eli's corrupt sons, Hophini and Phinehas. That would be like taking a coaching position where the previous coach taught bad fundamentals and had no discipline. Not only would they have to start from scratch, they would also have to correct an awful lot of previously learned bad behavior.

Samuel was able to bring Israel back to a proper worship and right standing with God as well as successfully hold the Philistines at bay. As long as Samuel was judge, the people were content to walk in the ways of the Lord. Their confidence and respect were once again restored.

Samuel was not a king. Nor was he even a

commanding officer in the army. He was a prophet of the Lord without fear or favor. He was God's chosen man. He did not have a palace or soldiers to force his will. Yet, his power and influence was life changing. His calling was ordained of the Lord, his speech was straight from the mouth of God, and the Word of the Lord was, through the office of the prophet, being conveyed to the people. His passion was for the spiritual health of Israel.

I believe that his love for God and God's people is why Samuel was chosen to anoint David, the greatest king to rule over Israel before the coming of Christ. Samuel had become God's mouthpiece because and his heart was connected to the will of God. To inquire of the Lord by Samuel was like hearing from the Lord personally. His faithfulness to God and the people was unmatched by any other.

Man-led kingdom instead of a God-led kingdom

When Samuel became old, he set up his sons Joel and Abiah to be Judges over Israel. They did not have the same love and passion for God or the people as their father had. They took bribes and misused their power for their own gain. Because of what had happen in the past with the two sons of Eli, the former judge of Israel, the people were ready for change. They did not want to go down that road again.

The elders of Israel assembled together at Ramah before Samuel to ask for a king to be set over them. Samuel had given his life in service to them. Now, they were asking for a change, a different type of leadership than a prophet or priest. They desired a secular king. This was overwhelming to Samuel. They were seeking the guidance of a man-led kingdom instead of a God-led kingdom. God knew how connected Samuel had become to the people. He spoke to him and said, "They have not rejected you, but they have rejected me." If it was not for the Lord telling Samuel to allow this, Samuel would have resisted it with his very last breath.

A leader to leaders!

It is easy to see that Samuel's priorities were in the best interest of the people. He instructed them in the way of the new government and also revealed the mannerisms of a king. He protested their request to show them that God was not pleased with their desire to have a man set over them, but he allowed them to choose.

Now that Israel was in search of a king, Samuel was intent on establishing an individual that would defend and lead Israel in a right direction. It was time for him to be removed from the main spotlight to be put behind the scene, or should I say to the sideline. Still in calling the plays, he was still the prophet that heard from God.

However, his immediate task was now to establish a secular leader for the people. Wow! A leader to leaders! It may have seemed like he was being demoted. But actually, in the spiritual realm, he had been promoted from a judge to the anointer of kings. His eyes were no longer on the people of Israel or their conduct per se, but on the leadership of Israel and its conduct.

Many businesses have a chain of command that starts with superintendent. Under him are supervisors and under them are lead men or department heads. At the bottom of the chain of command are the rank and file employees. If something goes wrong, the superintendent does not ask the employees what happened. He goes to the one to whom oversight of the people has been entrusted, the supervisor!

God's will is for us to be stewards of His kingdom. Samuel had been placed into a position of calling out and overseeing

Kings. This started with his desire to hear God's voice, to protect and rightly instruct the people. His faithfulness to the kingdom of God opened doors for him. When you are a business owner, the person you want to put over your company is someone who really cares about the product and the employees. You would choose someone who has bought into your vision for the future of the company, someone who would carry out your desires and manage with authority on your behalf.

Such was the position wherein God established Samuel, a place of overseeing power and authority given to others. Even though God actually chose the king, Samuel was chosen to pour the anointing oil upon God's chosen leader. Why did God use Samuel? Why didn't he just place his calling on the new king without Samuel even being present?

I believe it is God's desire not just to work through us, but to work with us and us with him. His Word says we are to be joint heirs with Christ. To me, this means God's will is for us to have oversight in the kingdom. We are called to be sons of God, not slaves of God.

Samuel was the current judge in Israel, put in that position by God. He was wholly following the Lord. I don't believe God would go behind his back and raise someone else up. He went through Samuel and, by his God given authority, the new king was anointed.

God is not a usurper, especially against His own Word.

This seems to be the avenue that God takes in dealing with mankind. He does not usurp the authority away from us but rather works through our abilities. God gave Adam and Eve authority over all creatures and the Earth.

And God said, "Let us make man in our

image, after our likeness: and let them have dominion over the fish of the sea, and over the fowl of the air, and over the cattle, and over all the earth, and over every creeping thing that creepeth upon the earth." (Gen 1:26 KJV)

He gave them this authority unconditionally. Even though they had sinned, they still had the authority. God did not go back on his Word to them. What God does here on Earth, he does through mankind in whom he gave authority. He will not usurp the authority that He gave to man like Satan did in the Garden of Eden when he deceived Eve into eating of the tree of knowledge of good and evil.

To save us from our sins, God had to work through mankind. He did not bypass His Word, the promise He had given to man. "But when the fullness of the time was come, God sent forth his Son, made of a woman, made under the law," (Gal 4:4 KJV)

If we look at the history of Israel and even the New Testament church, we see how God performed His will through mankind. Noah, Moses, Abraham, Samuel, David, Jesus, Peter, and Paul are just a few examples. The book of Revelations calls God a faithful witness. He works through the authority of His Word. If this was true in the Old Testament, then it is relevant for today. I surmise that God, at this very moment, is looking for some humans in whom to place His will and power so that His perfect will is carried out in the earth.

Sometimes it seems that Christians are waiting on God to do something when, in reality, it is God who is waiting and watching for believers who are willing to do something for the kingdom. God worked mightily through the apostles and he wants to work mightily through you and I.

An army and resources that supersede all others

What a great position to have stepped into where your every word comes to pass. Imagine being the individual God calls on to anoint leaders to rule over His people. To me, it is so awesome to think we can excel with God in such an incredible capacity. There must be a joining of wills where our desires become indistinguishable from His. Remember, Jesus said in the garden of Gethsemane before his crucifixion, "Not my will but thy will be done." Many wish and fantasize about possessing supernatural powers sort of like a Jedi knight, Spider Man, or Iron-Man or some other super hero with enhanced abilities greater than their own natural abilities.

The truth is that we do live in a supernatural realm as well as a natural one. There are mega forces coming against the people of God. Satan, the prince over the kingdom of darkness, is unleashing all kinds of demonic forces continuously.

"For we wrestle not against flesh and blood, but against principalities, against powers, against the rulers of the darkness of this world, against spiritual wickedness in high places." (Eph 6:22 KJV)

These demons are coming against all of mankind, not just believers. They are perverted powers who have one purpose, that is to bring chaos. Jesus said that Satan's intent is to kill, steal, and destroy. There are different levels of power in the demonic realm and some devils are more wicked than others.

"Then goeth he, and taketh with himself seven other spirits more wicked than himself, and they enter in and dwell there: and the last state of that man is worse than the first." (Matt 12:45a KJV)

There are spirits of fear, murder, suicide,

addiction and so on. Sad to say, many have no idea what they are up against. There are people who are misled into thinking they are gaining power by participating with destructive spirits, witches, soothsayers, Satanists, and others. In reality, such individuals are being used to deceive their fellow man into accompanying them on their own destructive way to being cast aside.

As the forces of darkness seem to have some power, the powers of the kingdom of God prove to be real and infinitely greater. Nations of the world compete to see who has the most power and authority, a commanding general of the United States Army, or a commanding general of Iceland's army? They both have power over their own army, but one has an army and resources that exceed the other.

Such is the case in God's kingdom which is far greater than Satan's kingdom and is founded upon reality, not deception and lies. The kingdom of righteousness is governed according to true principles that are effectual and lasting. Satan's kingdom is a misled, twisted, and perverted path that does not hold up for mankind. You cannot build your life on it. His kingdom is designed to destroy all of mankind.

The kingdom of darkness is comprised of those who have rebelled against righteousness and truth. It is not a true kingdom but is more like a cancerous cell. It started off being good and beneficial to the body but then went terminally bad until it became a diseased and mortal threat.

His honesty, faithfulness and love for God and Israel propelled him to power

Great heroes of faith and power don't come out of comic books. They step right out of the plan and purpose of God. Samuel was one such hero. He stepped into a place of anointing men to reign over God's heritage, the beloved children of Israel. He such a giant in stature that even the armies of the Philistines stopped challenging Israel while he was judge.

His honesty, faithfulness, and love for God and Israel propelled him to power and authority in the kingdom. Samuel commanded the people to repent of their transgressions against God, to uphold the ways of the Lord in great honor, and to assure fair and right judgment toward each other.

Then Samuel spoke to all the house of Israel, saying, "If you return to the Lord with all your hearts, then put away the foreign gods and the Ashtoreths from among you, and prepare your hearts for the Lord, and serve Him only; and He will deliver you from the hand of the Philistines." So the children of Israel put away the Baals and the Ashtoreths, and served the Lord only. And Samuel said, "Gather all Israel to Mizpah, and I will pray to the Lord for you."

So they gathered together at Mizpah, drew water, and poured it out before the Lord. And they fasted that day, and said there, "We have sinned against the Lord." And Samuel judged the children of Israel at Mizpah. (1 Sam 7:3-6 NKJV)

Power and prestige with God comes through loyalty. His kingdom deals in the eternity of human souls. God will not promote half-heartedness or a lack of commitment in his realm because the stakes are too high. Samuel was dedicated to the Lord from birth, raised in the temple as a prophet called by God and committed to Israel. His relationship with God was not just some temporary phase or whim. It was the passion of his heart and soul. To disobey God or misrepresent Him would have been high treason for Samuel. He was speaking not on his own behalf, but for God.

We pray and ask for power over the devil, to heal the sick, to change our community, and to excel in the kingdom of God. These prayers are right and proper. However, with the power comes the responsibility to represent the realm of heaven in a right manner.

Growing up in church all my life I have seen a few things take place that did not line up according to God's word or His will. I remember a revival I attended when I was a youth. It was at a church in a neighboring town and I went with my folks. The evangelist preached what seemed to be a powerful message. He talked about seeing angels and told about great things God had done in his life. Then, he took his coat off. He called it his mantel and threw it on the floor. He told the people to come and throw their offerings on it. Before the service was over he had placed his coat on the floor three times.

I never did see any angels or even see anyone healed in that meeting. The evangelist left after about four days of preaching and everyone was a lot poorer. No doubt, this man was in ministry to benefit himself and not the kingdom of God.

Are there true men and women of God with power to heal and bring deliverance today? Absolutely! I have seen people healed with mine own eyes. I saw several people healed under my dad's ministry and others. However, there are those who are like the above mentioned evangelist who put on a good show with no substance to their words or actions.

To walk in the power of God is to walk in the will of God

Everything Samuel spoke came to pass. His words must have been totally in line with God's will.

"And this is the confidence that we have in him, that if we ask anything according to his will, he heareth us: And if we know that he hear us, whatsoever we ask, we know that we have the petitions that we desired of him." (1 John 5:14-15 NKJV)

From the abundance of the heart the mouth speaks. His mind, soul, and spirit were sold out to God. Words are not just to be sounds we make in the wind. There must be something to enforce them. Jesus said, "The words I speak unto you they are spirit and they are life." When we speak, there is a force behind our words to cause things to come to pass, to manifest. It may be faith or love, but we can feel that emotion when the words are spoken. On the flip side, there are also spirits of fear, unbelief, and so on that bring destruction through words spoken with evil intent.

Jesus said, "You shall love the Lord your God with all your heart, with all your soul, and with all your mind." Samuel must have been totally committed to God with his whole being. It is impossible to speak as an oracle of God if we are half hearted in our relationship with Him.

The disciples said of Jesus, "What manner of man is this! For He commandeth even the winds and water, and they obey him." He no doubt was speaking with the omnipotent power of God. Samuel also spoke and said that God would send lightning's and thunder to show His disapproval of their asking for a king. It came to pass just as he said.

His desire was God's desire and God's desires were his. When our will comes in line with the will of God, we have power to do great things. What is the will of God? I do not know all the will of God. However, I can see part of His will clearly by the stories of the Bible. It is God's will that mankind come back to believing in Him. This is plain to see.

"For God so loved the world, which he gave his only begotten Son, that whosoever believeth in him should not perish, but have everlasting life." (John 3:16 KJV)

God loves all mankind. He uses every means to reach out to His creation. When we step into fulfilling the will of God toward humanity, then the power of His Spirit is present to fulfill His will through us. If Samuel was not speaking in agreement with the will of God, His words would have fallen. But, they came to pass just like he said. God backed up his every word.

To walk in the power of God is to walk in the will of God. He will not establish the words of a carnal man or back up the desires of the flesh. He will stand for truth and righteousness that He has established in the heavens, bringing His righteousness forth into the world. God's truth will prevail over the darkness that has come from the fall of man.

Samuel was a representation of this truth to Israel. Through the house of Eli the people had fallen into idolatry and sin. Their backsliding had caused them to lose their authority over the Philistines and other enemies that were in the land. They even lost the Ark of God, their most sacred possession, in battle.

God called!

In order to be a king-anointer there were some requirements to be met by Samuel. Even for you and I, the calling into the work of the kingdom is initiated by God himself! We cannot appoint ourselves to His work. Remember that Hannah was barren, unable to have a child. She prayed and the Lord enabled her to conceive. Hence, Samuel's birth was ordained of God.

Hannah went not up for she said unto her husband, "I will not go up until the child be weaned, and then I will bring him, that he may appear before the LORD, and there abide forever." And Elkanah her husband said unto her, "Do what seemeth thee good; tarry until thou have weaned him; only the LORD establish his word." (1 Sam 1:22- 23

KJV)

Committed to the work of God by his mother which was also approved by his father, young Samuel was dedicated and consecrated by a bull, flour, and wine. The Bull represented the blood, the flour was the bread or the Word, and wine was the Spirit.

The Lord also came to Samuel as a child and spoke with him. He revealed his plan of the future concerning the house of Eli, that his family would be punished and all male descendants of Eli would die before reaching old age.

Samuel was not a Levite. He was from the tribe of Ephraim, so he could not be a priest. He did grow up in the temple, but he was a prophet of the Lord, not a priest.

The Lord also appeared to him in Shiloh: for the Lord revealed himself to Samuel in Shiloh by the word of the Lord. Shiloh is where the tabernacle was set up; the Ark of the Covenant was there also. This was God's house at that time. God confirmed His Word to Samuel in the house of the Lord before the tabernacle of witness.

There also must be a commitment to the call of God. Samuel was set apart as a Nazarite to the Lord. No razor came upon his head. He grew up in the temple from the time he was weaned by his mother. He never faltered in his walk with the Lord. Psalm 99:6-7 says of Samuel, "Moses, and Aaron, they called upon the LORD, and he answered them. He spake unto them in the cloudy pillar. They kept his testimonies, and the ordinance that he gave them." These men were God's best!

Athletes who make it to the Olympics are the best in the world. As I was watching an 800-meter race, the announcer said of one young lady that she was the NCAA champion in that event. She was from the United States. I thought, "Wow she must be awesome!" But this was not an NCAA title match. This was the Olympics. When the race started, the young woman was fast. However, this time she was running against the best in the world. She kept up until the last lap of the race. Then there were three that began to turn the wheels on and pull away from the others. The young lady, our NCAA champion, placed fourth in the event.

The level of commitment it takes to be an Olympian is the highest level there is for athletes. To be a king-anointer is the highest level there is for a believer. This is not something we can obtain in the realm of mediocrity. It takes a totally sold out life like the prophet Samuel's.

In the sea of humans on the face of the earth today, there are chosen individuals that God has prepared for this time and hour. God is looking for Samuels that are going to step up and call out those individuals to positions of power and authority in the kingdom of God. The anointing to call out kings and priests will rest upon them and now is that time.

When Samuel poured the oil on David's head it was time for a change in leadership. Rise up church. It is time for us to shine with the glory and power of Jesus Christ. The forces of Darkness have come into the land. They are invading every area of our society even the church.

God's laws and statutes are being ignored in our government, schools, courts, homes and even in the Church where it is supposed to be the pillar and ground of the truth. If there ever was a time for obedient and committed servants like Samuel, it is now. There are young servants like David in the crowd now. It is time for that prophetic anointing to call them out.

Chapter Two
Among the Stuff

Now the LORD had told Samuel in his ear, saying, "Tomorrow about this time of day, I will send a man to you out of the land of Benjamin, and thou shalt anoint him to be captain over my people Israel, that he may save my people out of the hand of the Philistines: for I have looked upon my people, because their cry is come unto me." (1Sam 9:15-16 KJV)

God was preparing a deliverer for His people from their enemy – the Philistines. Believe me, Samuel was not going to anoint just anyone. The king had to be God selected and God approved. When Saul came to Samuel in land of Zuph he was looking for his father's mules. He was just trying to be a worthy steward of his father's possessions. He had no inkling of the encounter that was about to take place. One thing that I have detected about God encounters – they always transpire when we least anticipate them.

Samuel knew that day he would come into contact with the person God had chosen and was waiting for that person's arrival. When Saul met Samuel at the entrance of the city, he requested to see the seer. Samuel told him he was the seer and that his mules were found. Samuel proceeded in telling Saul that all the desire of Israel was on him. This bewildered Saul. He responded by saying,

"Am not I a Benjamite, of the smallest of the tribes of Israel? And my family the least of all the families of the tribe of Benjamin? Wherefore then speakest thou so to me?" (1 Sam 9:21 KJV)

His mind was settled on his inabilities instead on his possibilities.

These were foreign words to Saul. What! Come again! Shut up! Or some other interjections we might use today. I cannot imagine what was going on in Saul's mind. He was there only to recover his father's mules and then go back home to his father's farm where he belonged. Saul had what it took to be king, but he could not see that in himself. That was something he probably never even thought about. He said he was from the tribe of Benjamin – the smallest tribe of Israel. His view of himself, his family, and his people was inadequate for a position of such great importance. His mind was settled on his inabilities instead of his possibilities.

Why would God choose someone from such an insignificant tribe? Why would he pick his family? They weren't exceptional in any way, shape, or form. Why would God want to pick him? What Samuel said did not make sense to Saul because his image of himself was small. He had calculated into the equation who he was, who his family was, and what tribe he came from.

Benjamin was the smallest tribe in Israel; they had committed a horrible act that caused the other eleven tribes to war against them. This reduced their army to no more than six hundred soldiers. Benjamin was a very small tribe with not much physical abilities. Saul had established in his mind that he would just be a farmer like Kish, his father. That was his destiny and he was content with it. But, God had other ideas for Saul.

Inside of us there is the desire to be great. But, many times we lack the faith to become great. We love to dream or imagine of doing great things, but turning those dreams into reality is another story. We allow our destiny to become fixed in our minds based upon what is dictated to us by everything around us in the natural.

This has been the downfall of many. They look at their own self without the God-given abilities. It's kind of like going to buy a house when all you have is two thousand dollars. The realtor tells you the house you're looking at is one hundred and twenty thousand dollars. Your mind is like, "No way will I ever be able to live there! I only have two thousand dollars." The realtor, like all good realtors, informs you that if you have good credit, with two thousand dollars down you may be able to obtain a loan from the bank. Now you are factoring in your money along with the bank's money. Buying the house seems closer to becoming a reality.

Saul was looking at his qualifications and not what God's power and assistance could add to him. God's wealth of wisdom, strength, and power are unlimited. Your two thousand dollars may not be much when you're trying to buy a one hundred and twenty thousand dollar house. However, when you figure in the resources of the First National Bank, that brings excitement to the realtor.

There has to be a transfer from the servant mentality to a king mentality, but without losing the servant's heart

Samuel was thrilled about Saul's visit because the unlimited banker had already told him of His plans to finance Saul's kingship over Israel. All Saul had to do was just be obedient to the call. Even though Saul had confessed he was not worthy of this call, Samuel gathered the elders of the city together for a feast and set Saul in a position of great honor.

I would have loved to hear Saul's thoughts at that banquet. He was most likely thinking, "Wow! They think I'm someone else. Free food, and then my servant and I are out of here." Maybe he was thinking, "This guy, Samuel; his elevator must not go all the way to the top." One thing is for sure. He was not thinking he would be the first king of Israel. His view of himself was more that of a servant than a king.

To think of ourselves as a servant is right and appropriate. Keeping a humble heart and esteeming others more highly than ourselves is very important in order for us to keep a right perspective in life. Samuel told Saul years later, when his pride had taken over, that while he was small in his own sight he could be led and taught. If Saul could have known how to transfer from a servant mentality to a king mentality without losing the servant's heart, he would have been a great king for Israel.

Insecurity! It is a lack of confidence of who we are in God

When someone is elevated to a position of power and authority over others, the flesh has a tendency to be puffed up. Devoid of a good sense of who we are and where we started from, it becomes easy to lose sight of being a servant. If we are not careful, we can go from the view of being a servant to others, to the thinking of
others as servants to us.

One time I was listening to a person who used to be extremely famous. They said at first all was well. Then, they started getting involved in drugs and many other things that resulted in their downfall. He said that people were always telling him how great and wonderful he was to a point where he started believing it. Pride blinded his eyes and it was not long after that he started thinking he was invincible.

Saul's battle – Insecurity! It is likewise a battle for us today. It is a lack of confidence of who we are in God. Being insecure makes us feel naked or exposed. There is the overwhelming desire to cover up our weaknesses, so we may feel secure. A self-doubting person can easily fall to the ploys of Satan and even become a device he uses to bring separation to the body of Christ. Insecure people can be resentful of others, envious, prideful and so on.

Satan used Eve's self-doubt against her. God had made her for Adam. She was equipped to be his help mate. The role she was given was not to be the head, but a support to the head. In this she felt inferior to Adam. Satan knew precisely where to tempt her. He told her if she ate of the tree she would be wise. Since Eve was there when God told them that they could not eat of the tree of knowledge of good and evil, she had to discard the truth in her heart first before she could accept the propaganda that Satan was speaking.

Her insecurities initiated her to question her mental capabilities and prompted her to justify her licentious need for more knowledge. She was not even content with being mortal. She wanted to be like God, knowing good and evil.

There is only one true covering that we have to shield our nakedness and insecurities with. It is the covering of God's spirit. This is His spirit of truth that is sent down from above, available for all. Today, because of the work that Jesus Christ completed on the Cross, all who have accepted Jesus Christ as Lord and Savior have access to God's full covering for our body, soul, and spirit. Our hearts are to be committed to Christ and our soul covered by the Spirit of the Lord. Then we stand firm in truth and righteousness. The word says the righteous are bold as a lion, but the wicked flee when no man pursueth.

The Holy Ghost has no weakness at all. He is not bound by fear or lies. To put on the Lord Jesus Christ is to put on grace, power, confidence, and love. All have some sort of insecurity for we all have sinned. But, in Christ, we are made whole again.

Hid himself among the stuff

"Samuel called all Israel together at Mizpeh so that he could reveal who God had chosen to be king over Israel. When he had caused all the tribes of Israel to come near, the tribe of Benjamin was taken. When he had caused the tribe of Benjamin to come near by their families, the family of Matri was taken, and Saul the son of Kish was taken: and when they sought him, he could not be found. Therefore they inquired of the LORD further, if the man should yet come thither. And the LORD answered, Behold, he hath hid himself among the stuff." (1 Sam 10:21 KJV)

I suggest that we also would have hid among the stuff. Saul knew who was going to be taken. He perceived what was to be expected of him as king, what kind of accountabilities that would be required of him. What if he failed? What would people think of him? What if he did something that was totally stupid? He would be the laughing stock of all Israel.

It is always much easier to find an exit out of the limelight, someplace safe out of sight, than to step out and risk failure or disappointment in the eyes of everyone. To go much farther than we have ever been, is to move into the realm of the unknown.

That is a scary step.

We cannot remain frozen and immobile in our fears and insecurities. We must step into areas where we have never gone before. Turtles never get anywhere until they stick their necks out. Birds will never learn to fly until they get out of the nest. Abraham and Sarah ventured into a land where they had never dwelt before.

Many never move beyond what they perceive to be the extent of their abilities in order to experience incredible areas of greatness and fulfillment. Think of this for a moment. What stops us? Fear, doubt, or anxieties? Where do you think those feelings come from? Because we probably are looking at ourselves rather than looking to God Almighty. Or, we are so used to being controlled by others, told what to do and what to think, that it takes great courage to step out. We must be brave enough to take the risk. Before we will take the risk, we have to be sure it is worth it.

Many today are hid among the stuff. If there was ever a time for Godly leaders to stand up and take their place leading our nation, it is now. Many have buried themselves into those things that don't have any eternal value. We have become experts on everything under the sun, but are totally ignorant of what matters the
most – God's will for our lives and the operation of the Spirit!

When it comes to fighting for the souls of the lost, standing for truth, we just want to get our mules and go home. Or, we are so consumed by our stuff that we don't have time to do the work of God. It's hard. It's not easy. There is too much responsibility. What if we fail? What if no one wants to hear us? Our excuses go on and on.

The stuff has become a hiding place for those who are running from the call of God. He is wrestling with our souls to bring us to the responsibilities of saving the lost. Godly leadership is needed. The battle is set. Devils are devouring countless lives while so many God called kings and priests are hidden among the stuff.

Even though Saul was anointed king by Samuel, his fears kept him from completely trusting in the Lord. Because of this, he was unable to become the king that Israel needed. Lack of trust in the Lord keeps us from stepping into our full potential.

When our faith fails we fall into fear

Saul's lack of faith in his abilities and in the power of God caused him to pursue other means of support. He even became afraid when Samuel was not with him as the Philistincs gathcred themselves together to fight with Israel, thirty thousand chariots, six thousand horsemen, and people as the sand which is on the sea shore in multitude. Saul sacrificed unto the Lord and made supplications because he was sure he was going to die that day by the hand of the Philistines. When our faith fails we plummet into paralyzing fear. From this time forward, Saul could not stand before his adversaries. His son Jonathan or David his servant had to make the stance against the Philistines for him. His fear replicated his relationship with God. There is no fear in love, but perfect love casteth out fear because fear hath torment. He that feareth is not made perfect in love.

Saul's heart was not true toward God. This caused him to stumble in vital decisions as king of Israel. He compromised God's instructions to destroy all of the Amalekites. He allowed jealousy to come in through the door of his fears because he felt that the people desired David to be king instead of him.

Instead of keeping his faith in God's sustaining abilities, he allowed the apparent circumstances move him to make bad choices. So many make their decisions based on what they perceive with their eyes. Faith looks beyond the circumstances and looks to the supernatural, the realm of God's creative power to bring liberation to the believer. The things that are seen were made by the things that don't appear.

The unseen realm of the Spirit is more powerful than the material world before our eyes. God's Word has the ability to change the situation. Countless times, Israel was outnumbered in battle. However, with God's aid they became victorious.

In the last battle fought by Saul, he was prepared to go out and fight. He gathered all Israel together and pitched in Gelboa. But when he saw how huge the army of the Philistines was, he became afraid. This prompted him to seek out a source that was not of God. He wanted guidance but was not obedient. He wanted assurance, but God would not answer him because of his rebellion. Saul then went to the witch of Endor.

He was anointed king over God's people. He had prophesied among the prophets and won battles and conquered army's. But now he has allowed all of the self-doubt and fears bring him to Endor looking for some sort of hope that will save his own skin.

Because of rebellion and iniquity, many have found themselves separated from the voice of God. They are wandering in the land of Endor looking for guidance from the false spirits of this world.

Fear will make you flee from the battle and self-doubt will kill your faith

In retrospect we all have insecurities that we deal with. We are mortal, frail, weak human beings. This is who we are. We must have the Spirit of the Lord in order to stand against the onslaughts of the hostile atmosphere in which we live. Like sheep among wolves, no matter how tough we may feel, we are still no match for a wolf, let alone a pack of wolves. Sheep must have protection provided by a force that is greater than them. The Shepherd is the keeper and protector of the sheep. He stands guard over the sheep and leads them into places that are secure. The sheep must stay nearby the shepherd for their protection. We have a great shepherd that watches over us. He is with us at all times. We must place our confidence in the ability of the Word that He has spoken to us, trusting in His capabilities to accomplish His will and purpose in our lives while keeping us intact. We are all human, so why are some more insecure than others? The answer to that question is simple. It's their lack of faith in the shepherd.

For a great king of Israel, Saul's death was disappointing. He fled from the Philistines. He then fell on his own sword, taking his own life. Fear will make you flee from the battle, and self-doubt will kill your faith.

Chapter Three
Fill your Horn Again.

"And the LORD said unto Samuel, How long wilt thou mourn for Saul seeing I have rejected him from reigning over Israel? Fill thine horn with oil, and go, I will send thee to Jesse the Bethlehemite: for I have provided me a king among his sons." (1 Sam 16:1 KJV)

Samuel was greatly troubled by the actions of Saul because he had turned from wholly following the Lord. Samuel was in complete despair. What was he to do? He was the one who anointed Saul and ratified him in front of all Israel. Samuel was King Saul's personal advisor. He had invested his heart and soul into him ever since he was a young man so that Saul could be prepared to be a noble leader for Israel.

Saul used to be a follower of God's word, but now he was letting his own perspective to supersede God's will, pushing aside God's purpose and implementing what he felt was best for Israel. Saul was given plain instructions to fulfill judgment on the Amalekites for what they had done to Israel. God specifically told him, "Destroy everything. Do not leave anything alive."

Saul had allowed the people to spare any good thing that they took from the Amalekites and to destroy anything that was vile and useless. God's instructions have great eternal implications. The Amalekites had a curse upon them for coming against Abraham's seed. Also, God had given the land to Israel. They would be a fierce enemy and a hindrance to Israel if not annihilated.

"And I will bless them that bless thee, and curse him that curseth thee: and in thee shall all families of the earth be blessed." (Gen 12:3 KJV)

The sheep of the Amalekites that they

saved had a curse on them by God. Agag, the King who was spared to be a trophy, also had the judgement and wrath of God upon him. Saul had brought them back as a spoil. The battle was not Saul's. This fight belonged to the Lord. Saul was only to be an obedient instrument to accomplish the will of God.

God knows what's coming our way and He speaks directions into our lives

God was working toward establishing Israel as a kingdom that would last continually. His desire was for a leader to the people who would follow His guidelines to the letter, trusting wholly in His wisdom and guidance for Israel.

I played one of my son's video games and did very poorly at first. The game ended quickly. The next time I played I did better. This time I knew what obstacles were impending and positioned myself accordingly. God knows what's coming our way and he speaks directions into our lives so that we may place ourselves in a position to overcome.

Clay's favorite video game is football. He had one controller that messed up once in a while. His player would move to the right on its own. When that occurred he would unplug the controller and plug it back in. If that did not resolve the problem, he removed that controller and plugged in a different one.

A bad controller could cost him the game. God's work is so much more vital than a video game. We are talking about eternity and millions of souls. God was preparing Israel and Jerusalem for the coming of the Messiah and an eternal kingdom. His every command was strategically ordered for the development of the greatest kingdom ever to reign upon the face of the earth.

God's Spirit will always lead us according to the blueprint of His will.

We don't want to become a bad controller in the hands of almighty God. We don't want to be someone who disregards the voice of the Lord and sets out on their own course or obeys inconsistently, deciding for themselves what course of action is right.

I believe that God has great things in store for our lives. In order for someone to live out their God-given potential they must allow the Holy Spirit to lead them. God's spirit will always lead us according to the blueprint of His will.

Saul had rejected the voice of God in His heart. No longer would the Lord speak to him. He had forsaken the Lord and resorted to seeking an outside
source that was not of the Holy Spirit. He that hath an ear to hear, let him hear what the Spirit is speaking to the church. God is speaking. Are we listening or have we

tuned him out?

God has already arranged for the next stage

Samuel had to move on and not permit Saul's rebellion to hinder the plan of God for Israel. It was time for him to fill his horn with oil again and anoint someone else as king. Past failures can either prepare us for future success or derail us from moving onward.

"And Samuel said, How can I go? if Saul hear it, he will kill me. And the LORD said, Take an heifer with thee, and say, I am come to sacrifice to the LORD. And call Jesse to the sacrifice, and I will show thcc what thou shalt do: and thou shalt anoint unto me him whom I name unto thee." (1 Sam 16:2-3 KJV)

God had already arranged the next stage for His people Israel. Samuel's head was spinning but God was moving him forward.

It was not time to sit around and wonder what went wrong with Saul. Israel had to move forward. They were encircled by enemies and unity between the tribes was declining. Someone had to step up before Saul took Israel in a direction far from the will of God.

The wisdom of God secures us for tomorrow's manifestations.

Just as God had already made provision for Israel's new king, He has made provision also for our ministry in order to fulfill His will of winning lost souls to Christ. His Word says if we ask anything according to His will He hears us. I don't believe that He just gives us everything that we want. His promise to us is if we ask according to His will. Yes, He will help us in our personal needs also because He loves us just a natural father loves his child.

God's plans are always futuristic. His Spirit is preparing us for the next step or battle we may be facing. The wisdom of God is formulating perfect strategy and preparing us for tomorrow's manifestations. It is a fallacy to sit around and daydream about becoming a great high school football player when you have already graduated from high school. Even though some people waste a lot of time wishing they would have done things differently, God is in the business of creating and making all things new. He makes all things possible. God does not work in the fantasy or make-believe realm. He works in the manifestation of the supernatural.

Supernatural is outside of human ability. It comes to pass through the Spirit of the Lord. A fantasy is thinking of something that can never materialize by human efforts or by anything spiritual. God deals only with what can become reality. This is important for us to understand so that we do not waste our prayers on things that cannot come to pass. We must pray according to His will. To know His will is to know what His Word says.

New oil for a new king

The calling that is placed on the new king is just as significant as it was for the former king. The anointing oil is just as powerful as it was for Saul. With it comes heavenly authority and the covering of God's Spirit. Saul was lifted up and anointed to be the king of Israel. But he betrayed the calling and now God has chosen a new head for His people Israel.

Saul could only take Israel so far. Now it was time for someone else to take Israel to a higher level. It takes great faith to make it to great places. Saul did not have that in himself.

As Samuel filled his horn with oil, he knew it was for the anointing of a new king. No matter how much regret he felt in his heart, he discerned this was the right thing to do. He had previously taken hold of Saul's garment, ripping it, saying, "The LORD hath rent the kingdom of Israel from thee this day, and hath given it to a neighbour of thine, *that is* better than thou." (1 Sam. 15:28 KJV)

One evening my wife found a box of taco shells in the cabinet so she decided to fix tacos for dinner. Evidently they had got pushed to the back of the cabinet and had been there for some time. When she opened the box there was an unusual smell because the oil that the shells were cooked in was old. She could not use them any longer and had to toss them out.

New oil for a new king – the last one went bad and could not be used or trusted. If my wife would have used those shells it would have ruined the entire meal. If God allowed Saul to continue as king, his disobedience and half-heartedness would spread to all of Israel. By the time Saul died he had already killed some of God's priests, attempted to slay his own son Jonathan, and chased David, the captain of his army who had brought great victory to Israel, out of the country. Saul then sought the advice of a witch. And let's not forget about disobeying God's direct command concerning the Amalekites.

There is also an anointing for this generation

The new king would have to face the power and control of King Saul. There could not be two kings for Israel. A new king meant the end of the old and his reign. When change comes to a church there is always opposition, mostly from those who hold positions in the church. Often the old gaurd have allowed the mind and heart to grow cold to the Spirit of the Lord along with those who are currently in power. They fear they might lose their position or influence.

In the last ten years, the church in America and around the world has gone through such a change that it is practically unrecognizable. Just a few years ago most churches were very traditional, organized, and affiliated with a denomination. Today there has been a changing of the guard so to speak. A new generation has stepped up to the plate.

Things that the older saints held sacred are not that significant to the newer group who are getting behind the driver's seat of the leadership. For myself, I don't feel that I'm afraid of losing my control. But I am not willing to change and go in a direction that I know nothing about.

I guess it's kind of like a red winged blackbird trying to fly with Canadian geese. Their flight pattern is not the same at all, even though they are both going south for the winter. The geese fly much too high for the black birds and their honking only scares or confuses the red winged black birds. Our cultures and methods may be different. I may not understand the new, but I truly desire the will of God to bring myself and the next generation of believers to the place He has prepared for the church of tomorrow.

Just as there was a great anointing poured out on the day of Pentecost for the disciples and for those who were part of the Azusa Street revival in the early 1900s, there is also an anointing for this generation. It is just as powerful and needful nowadays as it was back then. God has already made provision for this generation to hear and receive the gospel of Jesus Christ. There are persons who have been selected for leadership by God and positioned to move the church to a place of success. They may not be in the limelight yet. But soon they will be called out to take their place.

Samuel was an advisor. Saul became an adversary.

The church is moving on. We can be a Samuel who is ready to fill our horns with oil for the next generation coming to power in the church, or we can be like Saul trying to stop any imagined threat to the status quo and rebelling against anything we feel is not suitable to our taste. To the new king, Samuel was an advisor. Saul became an adversary. What will you be to the up and coming believers who are ready to do something in the church?

The Gospel will stay the same. It's God's holy Word. But the culture is continually changing. May the grace of the Lord Jesus Christ give us the wisdom and knowledge for today to win souls for the kingdom of God.

Samuel had to carry the anointing oil to the new king. He feared opposition from Saul, but God instructed him to take a heifer with him and to make a sacrifice unto the Lord. While he is sacrificing he called Jesse and his sons to join him. There was a transformation getting ready to take place in the authority of the church, but it had to be done in a way that the flesh would not recognize it. The nature of man is prideful, selfish, sinful, and will quickly try to stomp out a real move of God.

Believe me when I say that there will be great opposition against the one who carries the anointing because he is called to establish a new and godly kingdom. Satan will do everything in his power to stop or greatly hinder the carrier of God's anointing. The power of God to establish a new and powerful kingdom is introduced by the yoke breaking anointing of God.

When Lee Harvey Oswald was aiming his 6.5 millimeter rifle out the window of the Dallas book depository, he was not aiming at the convertible that our president was riding in. He was aiming at John F Kennedy, the president of the United States. Why are we getting hit by the bullets of Satan's attacks? It is because of the anointing that we are carrying. The greater the anointing on our life the greater the attack will be.

But on the inside there is a heart after God.

God said to Samuel, "You go and make a sacrifice to the Lord. Call Jesse and his sons and I will do the rest." Don't focus on the division but on the provision. As Samuel was doing his godly duty according to the command of God, the Lord was working things out to fulfill His will. If we are not totally focused on submitting to the will of God in areas of change, we will end up allowing the flesh to stop what the Spirit is trying to do. Don't allow yourself to become discouraged. God will work it out. It may not be according to your plans, but it will work His way.

Saul represents the old man, the one whose mind has not been conformed to the Spirit of the Lord, the carnal mind. It chooses to follow the desire and reasoning of the human nature which self-rules and resists the Spirit of God. Samuel represents the guidance of God's Spirit, the Holy Ghost. The new king represents the new man who has been chosen to fulfill the will of God. This man does not have much in the way of the flesh, but on the inside there is a heart after God.

The LORD said unto Samuel, "How long wilt thou mourn for Saul?" In other words, let him go. He has chosen a direction which opposes the will of God. The future of Israel is at stake. Now get up and move on to those who are waiting to receive the anointing for the work of God.

This was a hard thing for me to learn as pastor. Don't sit around and mourn over individuals who have left the church or who will not get serious about their relationship with God. You cannot make people do the right thing anymore than Samuel could have made Saul obey the voice of God.

You are required to preach the truth and minister to others with all your heart. If they turn and leave, don't sit and beat yourself up over it. There are so many more that are ready and willing to receive the Word that you have for them. I have spent way too much time morning over those who just wanted to play church rather than getting real with God.

God has a great plan for the church. There are many that He has prepared to carry the anointing. They are there just waiting to be called out.

Chapter Four
Midst of his Brothers

And he said, "Peaceably: I am come to sacrifice unto the LORD: sanctify yourselves, and come with me to the sacrifice." And he sanctified Jesse and his sons, and called them to the sacrifice. And it came to pass, when they were come, that he looked on Eliab, and said, "surely the LORD'S anointed is before him." But the LORD said unto Samuel, "Look not on his countenance, or on the height of his stature; because I have refused him: for the LORD seeth not as man seeth; for man looketh on the outward appearance, but the LORD looketh on the heart." (1 Sam 16:5-7 KJV)

Samuel was looking for a new ruler for Israel, a strong and powerful individual who would be able to lead Israel. There would be much opposition that he would have to overcome. This new chosen leader would make Israel feel secure leading them as king.

When Eliab walked up to Samuel, he saw an authoritative looking man. Samuel assumed that if anyone could lead Israel, this man would be capable. He knew that the new king would have to face the fury of Saul in order to survive. Eliab seemed to be a worthy contender. But leadership takes more than physical capabilities. There must also be something greater than merely having a good head on your shoulders.

Look at our past presidents. The greatest ones were neither the smartest nor the strongest. It is said that Abraham Lincoln's education was comparable to that of an eighth grader. Franklin Roosevelt suffered a crippling disease that left him in a wheelchair. These two men brought our nation back from the brink of disaster.

Leaders must have a vision

There must be a heart of faith, determination and loyalty. The journey will get tuff! Times will come when strength and intelligence won't be adequate to pull you through. Eliab did not have what it took to be a godly and faithful king for Israel. The Lord had already scanned his heart. He told Samuel, "I have rejected him." It was not because of Eliab's exterior. He was not capable on the inside. He did not have the faith and courage that it took.

It never said anything about Eliab's sin or that he was unfaithful. He followed Saul to the battle against the Philistines. He must have been somewhat faithful and brave. But he did not have the faith and ability it would take to be king.

I like to play a good game of chess every once in a while. In chess there are sixteen pieces and not each of them has the same potential. The rook cannot move like the queen. Even though the rook is a very important piece, it can never be a queen. The rook is so much greater than the pawn. You would gladly sacrifice a pawn to capture a rook.

Even though the pawn has the least value, it has a potential to move to a position much greater than the rook. If the pawn survives to its journey to the opponent's side of the board, it can be transformed into any piece that it chooses – even a queen. The rook is a powerful piece, but it does not have that ability. Some are called to do great things and some are called to do greater things.

Leaders must have a vision, a goal, and a dream. Their ability to grasp the whole picture gives them the capability to make decent decisions at the right time. Diana and I were traveling to Pennsylvania from Kansas to visit her family. We were on Interstate 44 going through St. Louis, MO trying to get onto Interstate 70 east. I got stuck behind a semi-truck with a tall trailer. It was very difficult to see the signs for our turns because our vision was blocked by the semi. We ended up on the right road, but going the wrong way. We wanted the east route, but we turned on the west one. Eliab may have had some decent abilities but he did not have what it took to get Israel to the place that God had intended for them.

Vision has to be accompanied by faith in God's capability to equip us for the task to reach the goal. It is apparent that Eliab had physical capability, but he did not have faith for the mission. God saw something in his heart that was blocking his ability to lead Israel in the right direction. They would have ended up going the wrong way.

Jesse brought Abinadab and Shammah to Samuel. These were the three eldest and most physically developed sons he had. But the Lord told Samuel that they were not the ones. It appears that God had examined their hearts. It is clear to me that He knows who is faithful to Him and who will give in when the pressure's on.

God deliberately picked a fight with Satan over Job's faithfulness. All that Satan placed on Job, he could not cause him to curse God, or accuse God falsely. God knew his man and was willing to do battle with the devil over Job's devotion to him. Satan got thoroughly beat by a man from the land of Uz. God knows His people inside and out. Abinadab and Shammah, like Eliab, did not have what it took to be the next king of a God-called, God-anointed kingdom.

After Jesse's three eldest passed before Samuel, he had the rest of his sons pass by. But the Lord said neither had he chosen them. God did not want just anyone to fill the spot as king. He was looking for a certain someone whom he had prepared and selected from among the sons of Jesse. I guess you could say a special person in the midst of the others. Jesse's seven sons were fine and of great importance. But the person God desired had to be equipped for the calling at hand.

They would have to put the will of God above their own individual desires. When Samuel came to Bethlehem, it was big news! The town officials were visibly shaken over the visit. But where was Jesse's youngest son? He remained in the field to watch his father's sheep. His seven brothers had come to see the great prophet without him.

His obligation to his father was more important than his own preference or curiosity. Why didn't he just let one of the keepers watch the sheep for a while? But he remained with the sheep. There is a level of self-sacrifice in keeping sheep. Your focus has to be on their well-being and not on your own personal desires. Stuck out in the field away from the happenings of the town, to make a sacrifice like that indicated a sincere care for his father and the sheep.

He has the faith and courage to take Israel forward.

All of David's brothers were there to be presented to Samuel. It is apparent that they were seeking something greater than just being a caretaker of sheep. David's faithfulness to his father's sheep was so much that the seer had to send for him.

When Samuel saw Eliab he said, "Surely the Lord's anointed is standing before him." But when David stood before him, Samuel did not see a powerful looking person. God had to tell Samuel. And the LORD said, "Arise, anoint him: for this is he." David did not fit the criteria of a powerful king. He was young and handsome, not a rugged, weather-worn, battle scarred, and strong individual.

The real character is the unseen spirit in the heart. God knew inside of David was the heart and faith of a true king, someone who would be faithful in accomplishing the plan that was laid out for Israel. I can just hear God say, "That's him, Samuel, the one I have arranged to take Israel to the next level. He has the faith and courage to take Israel forward."

Saul had great abilities and even accomplished some victories, but to establish Israel as one of the most powerful kingdoms in the realm? Saul just did not have the commitment or confidence that he needed for the assignment. He struggled with insecurity and became fearful when the Philistines gathered against him. His son Jonathan had to lead the armies of Israel to victory.

Uncertainty is a crack in our faith

Saul gave into pressure by the people that initiated him to compromise the command of God to destroy all of the Amalekites. Uncertainty is a crack in our faith. When pressure is applied, our faith fails. I have a friend who worked for GE Jet Engine

Repair. Her job was to x-ray the blades on the engines. They spin at such a high rate of speed, if one would come loose it would be like a large bullet tearing through the jet. A hairline fracture in the blade would be devastating. The metal of each blade was x-rayed to see if there were any flaws in the metal that could not be picked up by the human eye.

In the same way, our hearts are being scanned as God ponders the heart. David may not have looked like a king on the outside, but he was healthy on the inside with no hidden cracks that might cause him to lose his faith when things got tough. The jet engine is what lifts the plain up off the ground and causes it to soar through the sky. If a defect was in one of the blades it could become the very thing that might cause the plane to crash.

The Lord had lifted Saul up to be king. But Saul's heart turned from completely following the Lord. The Lord said, "It repenteth me that I have set up Saul to be king: for he is turned back from following me, and hath not performed my commandments." Saul is coming apart and if someone does not take the helm, Israel will crash.

God does not waste any time. So right there in Bethlehem with the elders of the city, Jesse, and all of his sons present, Samuel, the prophet of God stood and raised his horn of oil over David's head. He poured it upon the young shepherd boy who would soon become the utmost king to ever rule over Israel.

Our family can be our greatest asset or our greatest adversary

This must have been mystifying to David's brothers. I believe at the time they were not sure what was taking place. But they would soon realize the impact of this get-together with the seer. The calling on their younger brother would alter the course of their lives as well as the lives of their children. I'm convinced that the God-calling that is placed on individuals surpasses all priorities and obligations in this life.

The sons of Jesse would no longer be referred to as "Jesse's sons" but they would be called "David's brothers." With no disrespect to Jesse, their father, his sons would afterwards be known by someone that all Israel would know, love, and respect. They would fight right alongside their little brother and even their sons. Some of them would become part of David's famous mighty men.

Eliab, Abinadab, Shammah, and the rest of his brothers were all present when David was anointed by Samuel. I don't think God was trying to rub it in their noses that he had chosen their little brother over them. I do believe he wanted them present because they would have a great part in helping David become the king of Israel.

Our family can be our greatest asset or our

greatest adversary depending on the condition of the heart. I can truly say that my family has been my greatest asset in my ministry. I know that without their help and support, I would not be able to do what I do.

David's family stood by his side when the king of Israel gave orders to have him killed. Was there jealousy among his brothers? Yes, but they did not turn against him. There were even times that David's family would save his life.

His family became his support system. They were there when he was first anointed by Samuel and they were there when he was installed as king over all Israel. Some of them were closer to him than others. God chooses whomever He wants whether we support the choice as a family or not. If God raises up one above the others, join in. Then the whole family is raised up together in honor and power.

At that meeting in Bethlehem I would assume if the Spirit of the Lord was speaking to the hearts of David's brothers, He would probably say something like this; "He is the one I have chosen to be king, now I have appointed you to guard his life from attacks. He is your brother you are his protectors. Now go and support the calling that is placed on his life to the best off your ability and I will bless you and your children for supporting my will for Israel."

God must have expected Cain to know the whereabouts of his brother Abel

A family must be a unit. There is strength in numbers, but if they are alienated they become weak. When Cain slew Abel and God asked Cain, "Where is your brother, Abel?" God must have expected Cain to know the whereabouts of his own brother. Cain's reply, "Am I my brother's keeper?" In other words he was saying, "We are not a team, I am not accountable for his health or safety. If he lives or dies what is that to me?"

David's brothers had the choice to link into the calling that was placed on their younger brother or they could have rejected the high calling that was place on him. David was a gift from God to his brothers and to Israel, just as Joseph was a gift to Jacob's eleven sons. God used him to preserve their lives. There are gifted people in the midst of every family. It is up to us to recognize them and place our support squarely behind them.

As soon as David was anointed by Samuel to be king over Israel, the Spirit of the Lord left Saul. There is anointing placed on persons for the position to which they are called. The anointing of Israel's king now rested on Jesse's son David.

The family that supports the one whom God has chosen will rise with the one that God has chosen

God's favor was squarely on Jesse's youngest son. This was a great blessing and an honor not just for David, but to all of his brothers also. They would soon be the family of the King of Israel. Doors of leadership, power, and prestige would now be opened to them and their children because of the call that had been placed on David.

Chapter Five
Keeper of Sheep or Searcher of Mules

"And Eliab, his eldest brother, heard when he spake unto the men; and Eliab's anger was kindled against David, and he said, Why camest thou down hither? and with whom hast thou left those few sheep in the wilderness?" (1 Sam 17:28a KJV)

It was apparent that David played his harp to his sheep. Therefore Saul sent word to Jesse and said, "Send me your son David that is with the sheep." So those who spoke to Saul about David knew that he played the harp and watched sheep. They must have heard him playing it in the field. Perhaps this was a pastime for him while he watched the sheep or it could have been something to comfort the sheep.

There was a certain care David had for his

sheep, staying with them while others went to the big events and taking time to play his harp to them. When war broke out and his brothers went to the battle, David stayed behind and made sure they were taken care of. One thing is for sure, David spent plenty of time with his father's sheep. In those days it was pretty much an open range. Shepherds would stay with their flocks twenty-four seven. David would be their soul provider and protector. There were plenty of dangers to guard against.

Who is this uncircumcised Philistine

The Philistines marched into Israel to do battle. When Saul received word, he gathered an army together and met the Philistines at Shochoh. Jesse's three oldest sons followed Saul to the battle. David returned back to the field in order to feed his father's sheep. It seemed his heart was more on who would maintain the sheep rather than what was happening at Shochoh.

The battle had come to a stalemate. The Philistines had a champion who was challenging anyone who would dare to fight him and no one wanted to stand up to the challenge of this giant. Jesse called David in from tending the sheep and told him to take provisions for his brothers and to check on their wellbeing. So, David arose early the next morning and left the sheep in the care of a keeper. The sheep were a concern of his. He would not have just left them to fend for themselves. He made sure they had protection.

When David arrived at the battle it was while the army of Israel was setting themselves up against an inevitable Philistine attack. They were shouting with a great shout to lift each other's spirits. The atmosphere was electrified. David, having located his brothers, pressed though the army and greeted them.

As David was talking with his brothers, the Philistine champion, Goliath, came forward and began to defy the army of Israel. David heard the Philistine and saw the reaction of Israel's army fleeing away from the Philistine in fear. As the soldiers spoke to one another, David said out of boldness, "What will happen to the man that kills this Philistine and takes away this reproach off of Israel?" The people tell him what the king will do for the champion who will stand up to him.

David spoke to the men that stood by him, saying, "What shall be done to the man that killeth this Philistine, and taketh away the reproach from Israel? for who is this uncircumcised Philistine, that he should defy the armies of the living God?"   (1 Sam 17:25 KJV)

When the Philistine spoke cursing, the spirit of Israel turned to fear, except for David. His spirit became angry, "Who is this uncircumcised Philistine?" What did he say against God's chosen people?" In David's mind this blasphemer would not see the sunset ever again.

David's speech angered Eliab who reprimanded David for his words. He classified him as a mischievous child and pointed him back home to his insignificant job of watching those few sheep in the wilderness. In other words, "Quit popping off, little punk, and head home to your diminutive job of watching sheep!"

Was his big brother irritated that he was there? No. I don't think so. He was probably glad to receive those things David brought. But the words of David made him and the others look like cowards because, while David had righteous indignation, they were cowering with fear and apprehension which are the opposite of faith. When the Philistine came out and stood, they actually ran and hid.

Eliab tells his little brother, "This is no place for a young, wet behind the ears sheep boy. Watching the sheep, to David, was a great responsibility. Evidently, to Eliab it was not. That's why he was the first to appear before

Samuel and to follow Saul to the battle. David had put the sheep first and even jeopardized his own life taking care of them.

Christ our Good Shepherd

Like David was for Jesse's sheep, Jesus is the Good Shepherd of you and I who are His Father's sheep. Pastors are also called shepherds. Whether they are good shepherds or not depends on how much they care about the sheep. David was willing to risk his life for the sheep, even pulling a lamb out of the mouth of a lion.

Sheep have many enemies. They are meat to all carnivores and there are a variety including wolves that run in packs, lions with ferrous claws and teeth, and powerful bears, all of which could easily overpower a shepherd. The body of Christ is referred to as the sheepfold. Jesus, of course, is the chief shepherd. And then there are shepherds over his flocks called pastors or elders.

Like shepherds, pastors also have to deal with threats to their flocks. David spent most of his time with the flock. Sometimes he was called out for special events or duties. But he always went right back to the flock. On the other hand, his brothers were not as committed. They were quick to look for other areas of personal interest. It is impossible to do a good job herding sheep if you're not there with the sheep. They depend entirely upon the shepherd. Sheep are followers. They must rely on outside sources for protection and guidance.

And David said unto Saul, "Thy servant kept his father's sheep, and there came a lion, and a bear, and took a lamb out of the flock: And I went out after him, and smote him, and delivered it out of his mouth: and when he arose against me, I caught him by his beard, and smote him, and slew him." (1 Sam 17 34-35 KJV)

In order for the flock to stay together and

not be scattered, there must be a guardian. Notice that David said the lion took a lamb - meaning a young sheep, an easy catch. Christians are most susceptible when they are new in the Lord. They don't know how to protect themselves against the attacks of the devil. This is why God has positioned shepherds over the flock. The lion had the lamb in his mouth. I've noticed that Satan will try to overwhelm new believers with words of fear and doubt that can leave them crushed. But David went and took the lamb out of the lion's mouth. God has empowered his servants to rescue the sheep from the attacks of fear and doubt. As a pastor, you must safeguard new believers from verbal attacks. They are not able to withstand them like those who are mature enough to recognize the devices of the enemy.

Satan wants to control people's lives. When David took the lamb out of the lion's mouth it turned on him. Make a stand against demons that are attacking others and they will turn on you. This is where complete commitment comes in. Jesus said the hireling sees the wolf coming and flees because he is a hireling. He has no real investment in the sheep. Those who are in it for self-gratification this is approximately how far they take it. They come under attack and it's time to load up the kids and head home. As long as they just sit and play the harp and worship in the moonlight all is well. But when they are attacked, they run for the hills and leave the sheep to fend for themselves.

We must be aware of the attacks of Satan

The greatest thing that prepared me for pastoring was growing up in a pastor's home. I saw firsthand the spiritual warfare my parents went through. Where the sheep congregate, there will always be wolves or even more ferocious predators. A hireling would flee when he saw a wolf. But, on separate occasions, David stood against a lion and a bear, slaying them both. When they rose up against him, he probably had no choice but to kill them. Or maybe David, like my dad keeping coyotes away from his chickens, understood that if he let them go they would be back and he would have to deal with them again. Instead of truly defeating the devil, we just run him off for a little while and it's not long before we are dealing with the same problem all over again.

David grabbed the lion by the beard, indicating he came straight at David with his teeth. Satan tries to quickly bite into vital areas of our life. To grab him by the beard is to control his mouth and evade his piercing teeth. Don't allow the enemy to speak into your heart. Take every thought captive.

Satan goes about as a roaring lion seeking whom he may devour. Attacks of the enemy must be taken seriously. When a boxer steps into the ring he has to prepare physically and mentally for the bout. If not adequately trained and prepared, he will be knocked out. To stand against the wiles of the devil, we must keep ourselves spiritually prepared. Jude said, "Build yourselves upon your most holy faith praying in the Holy Ghost."

The boxer is usually taken out by the punch he doesn't see. Satan's attacks are sneaky invasions that you very rarely see coming. But if you know that there is a tiger in the bush you will be on guard because even though you can't see him, you know he is there. It's when we start feeling safe and forget how deceptive Satan is that our guard is let down. He is waiting for that opportunity to attack.

David was a keeper of sheep, but Saul was a searcher of mules

David had a faithful spirit with the same care and commitment to his father's sheep as he would later exhibit toward the armies of his heavenly Father. He said to King Saul, "Thy servant slew both the lion and the bear: and this uncircumcised Philistine shall be as one of them, seeing he hath defied the armies of the living God." (1 Sam 17:36 KJV)

The lion and the bear were a threat to the sheep and he dealt with them. This Philistine was a threat to God's army and he was ready to deal with him also. Whatever he had to do, he would do fully confident that God was able to keep him from harm.

As long as David kept the sheep they were safe and secure. When we first heard of Saul, he was searching for his father's mules. Someone did not keep a close eye on them and they got away. Saul came into contact with Samuel to see if he could give him insight on where to find his father's mules.

Leadership is broken down into two groups, leading the willing and leading the unwilling. David was a keeper of sheep but Saul was a searcher of mules. The word sheep in the Hebrew means "one that follows." They desperately need guidance, protection, and direction. Mules, on the other hand, are totally different animals. You have heard the phrase "stubborn as a mule." The word mule in Hebrew means "breakthrough" to "spread or separate". They are self-willed animals. You have to drive them not lead them.

Sometime mules want to be sheep and sheep want to be mules

People's spirits are somewhat comparable. Either they are willing to be led or they are unwilling. Saul spent much time searching for his father's mules. Don't permit yourself to be consumed chasing mules all over the country. Shepherding people takes skill on your part and willingness on their part. For people to become humble like sheep, God's spirit must first be birthed into their hearts. Second, they have to come to the point where they want to be pastored. Not all believers want to be followers. Some have chosen to go their own way. Finally, Samuel has to inform Saul that his mules have been found. Sometimes they have to just go their own way for a while. No matter what you try, their minds are made up. Hopefully they will be found or they will come back to a place where the shepherd can reach them.

Mules can be frustrating to those who are keeping them. David fought off the lion and the bear to save the flock. Just imagine if they were mules instead of sheep. While he was fighting with the lion the mules might have seen it as an opportunity to escape. In this scenario, when David had finally slain the lion, he might have turned around to see that the mules were long gone. Pastoring people can sometimes be heartbreaking. After you have done all you can possibly do for people, they simply walk out on you. Sheep, on the other hand, stay with the shepherd. A good shepherd makes good sheep and good sheep make good shepherds even better shepherds.

Sometimes mules want to be sheep and sheep want to be mules. Mules occasionally yield themselves to be led, even though it is only a temporary state of willingness. Sheep belonging to Jesus have the tendency to go their own way from time to time also. This depends on the spiritual condition of the heart and it can hinge on whether or not they have faith in the shepherd assigned to lead them.

David was prepared to lay down his life for the armies of Israel while he was just a shepherd boy. He didn't even own a sword. Saul, on the other hand, had armor and skill in battle. He was a head higher than everyone else. But he would not risk going against the Philistine champion. After David slew the giant, the Israelites were prepared to make him the captain of their army. Israelite women met him coming from the battles and sang, "Saul has killed his thousands and David has killed his ten thousands," indicating David was ten times more courageous than Saul.

Saul stood out in the crowd but David stepped out of the crowd

They were ready to follow someone who jeopardized his own life to save theirs. Also, they knew that only someone who was empowered by God could have slain the giant. Saul stood out in the crowd, but David stepped out of the crowd. The Philistine defied Israel for forty days. All he saw was a crowd of scared soldiers until David showed up on that day. Then he saw a young shepherd boy step out from among the crowd.

When you step out by faith, I guarantee the enemy will try to run you right back into the crowed or slaughter you in front of everyone around so that you will be an example of futility and defeat to anyone who might get the nerve to stand up to him.

Dwelling in fear will never bring down the strongholds of the enemy. You must step forward in faith by the power of the Holy Ghost to win the victory. David knew when he stepped out against the giant that God went with him. When you step out from the crowd you will become the target of the devil. That's why many don't attempt to step out.

David said, "Moreover, The LORD that delivered me out of the paw of the lion, and out of the paw of the bear. He will deliver me out of the hand of this Philistine. And Saul said unto David, Go, and the LORD be with thee." (1 Sam 17:37 KJV)

Sheep will follow the ones they trust

Even Saul's own son Jonathan was shaken by his Dad's inabilities. He had to take it upon himself to defeat the Philistines at Gibeah when Saul, his father, was too fearful to go out against them. Jonathan also said his father had done foolishly by placing a curse on anyone who ate on the day of the battle. If they would have been able to eat and energize themselves, they could have utterly defeated the Philistines. When Jonathan saw David's faith and courage, he was ready to pledge his allegiance to him.

Sheep will follow the ones they trust. Jesus said, "My sheep know my voice, and they will not follow another." Mules, on the other hand, have their own itinerary. Sometimes they will follow and sometimes they won't. Winning the confidence of the people is a must to be able to move forward in your vision for the church. If you don't have their confidence, you will spend most of your valuable time searching for your lost, uncommitted congregation.

A keeper is someone who has accepted stewardship over something. A searcher is someone who has lost something or cannot find something formerly in his possession. Once he finds what he seeks he is no longer a searcher. He is then a keeper. David had something that none of the soldiers in Saul's army had. Saul was searching again looking for someone who would stand up to the giant. He even offered a great reward to the one who slew the Philistine.

There are those who do not have the faith to face their own battles. They are constantly seeking someone who will fight their battles for them. Saul even spread the word that he would reward whoever was willing to go out and fight against the Philistine. When David said to Saul, "I will go out and fight this Philistine," he offered David his armor to wear.

They are not to believe for us, but to believe with us

Can you visualize someone saying to you, "There is a slayer out there. Here, take my sword and my armor. You go out and fight with him while I hide here where it is safe." Now let's add more to it. What if the person wanting you to go out and fight his battle is a bulky well-built warrior and you are just a lad. That just doesn't make sense! Well that's exactly what Saul was doing. He put his battle on the shoulders of David. He did not have the faith to go out and fight for himself, so he was looking for someone who would do it for him. He even offered a reward.

We may look at Saul and think in our minds, "What a chicken." I don't think we need to judge him too quickly. Today, there are many who are doing the same thing. They are looking for someone else to fight their battles or have faith for them because they can't believe for themselves.

I do believe in the gifts of the Spirit and the working of miracles. I know there are those that God has called into distinct areas of healings and prophecy. That is evident in the Scriptures. But there is a point where we must have faith for ourselves. I cannot spend the rest of my life running around looking for someone to lay their hands on me or for someone to give me a word.

The battles that I face are for me to overcome. Many times we want others to believe for our healing and deliverance. Is it wrong for us to ask others for prayer? Not at all. However, they are not to believe for us, but to believe with us. There are times when we do need someone to come along with special gifts to help us or empower us. But the majority of the time it should be our own faith that carries us through. If not, we will spend our time and money looking for someone to come and lift us up instead of trying to lift our own selves up.

We can be a brave king in a palace or a brave shepherd in the wilderness

When David heard the Philistine defy God's people, he did not look around to see who was brave enough to stand up to him. He was instantly prepared to go out and do battle. He had the faith and courage to take the Philistine. There is an art to keeping something that you have. If you don't have the heart and skill, you will soon be a searcher again.

Eliab regarded keeping sheep as insignificant. He also stated the place where the sheep were, "in the wilderness." In other words, a menial task in an invalid place. On the other hand, he viewed himself as a mighty warrior in King Saul's army. He felt his position of standing on the front lines against the evil Philistines was so much more than watching a few sheep in the wilderness. Our position does not make us courageous. We can be a coward in the field with sheep or in the midst of a well-equipped army. We can be a brave king in a palace or a brave shepherd in the wilderness. Man looks at outward appearance, but God looks within the heart. David was not in Saul's army. But he was the only one who stepped out to face the Philistine.

David was brave not because he was a keeper of sheep, but because of who he was on the inside. He was faithful, committed to his father and to his God. Therefore, he displayed courage in everything that was placed under his hand. David had a courageous spirit. That's why God told Samuel when David walked up
to him, "Arise. Take your horn and pour the oil upon his head." There in front of Samuel stood the most powerful man in all of Israel in the form of a shepherd boy.

We may not be a soldier on the battlefield, but that does not mean we're not a courageous person. There are many brave people in all areas of life, the father who will give all to sustain his family, the 110 pound mom who would take on a whole mob to save her child, or a teacher who gives her life to save her students from a crazed gunman.

Chapter Six
The bigger they are, the Harder they Fall

"And David put his hand in his bag, and took thence a stone, and slangs it, and smote the Philistine in his forehead that the stone sunk into his forehead; and he fell upon his face to the earth." (1 Samuel 17:49 KJV)

I remember having trouble with a bully in my grade school. I told my dad how big the kid was that was picking on me. My dad's reply was "the bigger they are the harder they fall." It may not be the best advice in the world, but it did get the point across to me. I was not to allow the size of the threat scare me.

When the soldiers of the army of Israel saw the size of Goliath, they fled from him and were sore afraid. But David, unlike the

army, was not intimidated at all by Goliath's size or the malicious words that he spoke. I can just imagine my dad's words echoing through David's head - the bigger they are the harder they fall. Considering the great victory of a young shepherd boy in the valley of Elah was
likely the source from whence my dad got his saying.

We played a basketball team from Lebanon and I remember the game well. We lost it before we even got out of the locker room. The other team was good. they knew it and we knew it. I remember the attitude before we went out wondering if we were quite ready to get our tails whipped.

Your faith must be larger than the threat!

When David went down to the camp of Israel, he went down to see God's mighty army of Israel in whom he took great pride and had firm confidence. He was especially proud of his older brothers. He quickly ran up to them and saluted. When Goliath spoke against Israel's army, David said, "Who is this uncircumcised Philistine that he would defy the armies of Israel?"

Goliath's words were a slap in the face to David. When someone says something against what you believe in with all your heart, you cannot just sit there and take it. Something on the inside rises up. Now if David's faith was weak and his expectation for Israel was low, the words of Goliath would have subdued his will to fight. But David's hope for God's people was much greater than some Philistine with a big mouth.

I remember the words of Evander Holyfield before he fought Mike Tyson. He said Tyson was a bully and that he would just have to be a bigger bully than he was. When Goliath saw David he talked down to him. But it did not deter the shepherd boy at all. He spoke right back at Goliath and said, "You come to me with sword and shield, but I come to you in the name of the Lord of Hosts whom you have defiled." David's words were not just idle talk, but words of power backed up by God himself. He stated to Goliath that in his pride and disrespect, he had spoken against the creator of heaven and earth. By the power of God that was on his side, David would fulfill the wrath of God on Goliath and on the host of the Philistines so that everyone would know who God stood for.

It is clear that the Philistines thought they had presented a champion that no one could defeat. Their whole campaign was centered on Goliath. For when they saw that he was defeated, they tucked in their tails and ran back to their own country. One thing I have realized about Satan and his way of attacking God's people is that he will come at us with what seems to be an overwhelming force. Most of Satan's attacks are simply propaganda.

Fear is the main weapon he uses against us, just as the male lion roars to scare his prey into the trap of the lionesses. When the children of Israel first saw Goliath, fear took over and they fled away from him. Goliath had Israel's army paralyzed and he hadn't even defeated anyone yet. If we look at the facts here, Goliath never won a battle. He lost to the first person he fought. In the rank of the Philistines he was a champion. But standing against the people of God he was a loser.

Well, this brings me to a question. Does Satan have power? The answer to that question is yes and no. He definitely does among the lost. Goliath was a champion among his own people. But against Israel he was a loser. Satan has power in the children of disobedience. But against God's people he has none. It's when we, the people of God, allow the propaganda of the enemy to create fear in us that he is able to keep us bound.

On the battlefield Goliath was considered the champion. David was looked at as a mere lad. But in reality Goliath had not defeated any Israelites whereas David had slain a lion and a bear. He was the real champion on the field.

Jesus Christ, like David, defeated the dreaded enemy of our souls. We have victory over the whole host of the enemy's army through Jesus Christ. Goliath is a type of Satan and the Philistines are a type of all demonic principalities and powers of darkness. David is a type of Christ who came to slay the giant that stands in our way. As David defeated Goliath so Christ defeated Satan.

The stone that smote Goliath in the head represented the Word of God. Just as Jesus used the Word to overcome Satan's temptation in the wilderness, David used a sling and a stone to smite the giant. The stone sunk into the head of Goliath. Jesus' words pierced the mindset of sin that rained over us. Like the giant, Satan also fell on his face from a blow to his power and dominion over mankind.

The devices that are used against us usually become the key to our deliverance

There was no sword in David's hand. He ran and stood upon Goliath while he took Goliath's sword out of his sheath and cut his head off. Goliath did not even have a chance to pull it out. He came toward David with a spear and shield. His sword was there in case he needed it. But David was the one who needed it. David is quoted as saying, "There is no sword like that one." The Philistine had made it especially for their champion. They had no idea that it was the very tool that was going to be used to cut Goliath's head off and end his life.

God specializes in turning Satan's devices against himself. Haman hung on the gallows that he had built for Mordecai the

Jew. The president and princes of Babylon were eaten by the very lions they had hoped would eat Daniel.

The devices that are used against us usually become the key to our deliverance. They used nails on Jesus' hands and a whip on His back. To a cross was He nailed. Now to us, those nail prints mean salvation and the whip marks healing. The cross is the power of God over this old man. Our flesh is crucified and no longer has preeminence over us.

Jesus did not put those wooded nails into his hand neither did He place those stripes on His back or hang himself on that Cross. But those three things have proven to be our victory over death, hell, and the grave. Satan played right into God's hands.

The attacks that are coming against you are coming from the enemy. You may not see it now, but that will be the tool that is used to make you the godly person in Christ

Jesus that you were intended to be. I'm talking about those who are suffering persecution for righteousness sake, not those who are suffering because they have a wicked and unconverted heart.

David took full authority over the giant. He ran and stood upon him, "Satan, you are under my feet." Laying on the ground was the champion bully who, just a few minutes ago, had been cursing God's people along with David, God's chosen man. Now, he was lying flat on his face with God's man standing on his back, the giant's own sword in David's hand. I believe this is the proper place of the children of righteousness.

So many times we find ourselves in the opposite position, flat on our face with the devil on our backs. This is not the will of God for His people. Jesus said, "Behold, I give unto you power to tread on serpents and scorpions, and over all the power of the enemy: and nothing shall by any means hurt you."

David's stone is what knocked Goliath out, but it was the giant's own sword that David used to slay him. God's Word exposes all unrighteousness. But Satan is defeated by his own warped ways. Goliath had not even taken his sword out of the sheath. He probably came at David with the spear and was planning on using the sword to finish him off.

You cannot stop Satan from starting a fight with you. But you can defeat him. When you are attacked, your first position is defensive until you are able to get the upper hand. Once you have the upper hand you are still defending, but have switched the battle to where he is one that's on the ropes with his guard up. It's hard to punch and guard at the same time. Satan tries to keep us in a position of guarding ourselves so we cannot tear his strongholds down. It's not how you go
into the fight that counts. It is how you come out that matters.

You will be pulled into many battles by the devil. In order to win, at some point you must switch from defending to attacking. When my dad would pray, he always prayed with victory or attacking prayer. He had fought the fight and he knew how to pray.

I feel many believers pray the prayer of desperation "Help me oh God. Satan's got me by the throat and is about ready to cut my head off." That is a defensive prayer which will be our first prayer. But at some point it must be switched to, "I thank you Lord for making me a child of the king. You said in Your Word, *"Behold, I give unto you power to tread on serpents and scorpions, and over all the power of the enemy: and nothing shall by any means hurt you." (Luke 10:19 KJV)*

Remember Satan's thinking is warped because of sin. Devices that he uses against you can be defeated by the power and wisdom of God. He thinks he can control or bind you and he can if you give into his warped ways of doubt, fear, and unbelief. A person that has faith in God believes in himself and feels he has purpose. He can do great things for the kingdom and God. Those who give into the lies of the devil lose these God-given gifts and allow themselves to be bound. They feel inadequate, unfulfilled, and unable.

Their work becomes limited by their warped perspective. Satan has bound their minds so that they are bound in their abilities. There are many who are physically able to accomplish great things. But they live a defeated life in their mind. If you could only get them to see that they can do it. That's where Satan disables us, in our minds. Then we can't see ourselves for who we are and what we can do. It's easy to see others and identify them, but not our own potential and purpose.

"I can do all things through Christ which strengtheneth me." Just consider the man that made this statement. He was in a constant battle, war within, war with false brethren, war with the Jews, and so on. He still accomplished unbelievable tasks.

King Saul was a great person and soldier, but he allowed fear to bind him. If anyone could have defeated Goliath he could have done it. His faith in God had grown weak to such an extent that he no longer fulfilled all of His will. His insecurities caused him to rely on others for decisions that he was supposed to make.

Let's analyze Goliath for a minute. He was capable and he knew it. He said, "Choose you a man for you, and let him come down to me if he be able to fight with me." He was not afraid to stand in front of the army of Israel and defy them. He also was not afraid to speak out against the God of Israel. Some are bound in their abilities. Goliath was bound in his knowledge. He had no idea who he was speaking out against. Even though he did it with boldness, he died with shame and humiliation in front of all Israel and his fellow soldiers.

I hate to admit it, but Hitler was a military mastermind. He brought Europe to its knees. If it had not been for the Allied forces stepping in, he would have taken control. His downfall was his warped motives. Pride had blinded his eyes, puffing up his view of himself and the German people. In the end it cost him his life and the lives of many others.

We must have a right perspective of who we are in Christ in order to maintain a course that will end in success. Many have tried and failed because they relied on their own self-assurance and self-knowledge rather than relying on God. David had a great love for God and the people of Israel. He immediately spoke against anything that opposed that.

David did not see a giant. He saw a threat

to Israel's faith and to the one who had made them great, their God. He was ready to stand up for his God and country. We, as the body of Christ, have put up with too much from the devil. He's been speaking against God's people and God's authority. Yet we've stood passively on the side line.

The attacks of Satan can be overwhelming at times, but remember this. Fierce attacks come when there is much at stake. The greater the attack, the greater the victory will be.

Since I live close to Wichita, Kansas, I was rooting for Shockers basketball team in the NCAA tournament. Their first game was against #8 Pitt. The Shocks were ranked #9. The battle was tough, but they got the win and moved up in the bracket. Their next opponent was the #1 ranked team in their bracket – Gonzaga. This game was even tougher. There was more at stake here and they faced a much better team. WSU had to play to their best potential to win. They moved on up and played La Sal to advance to the Elite 8. Then they faced #2 Ohio State. The winner got to move to the final four of the tournament. Each time they won they moved up in the bracket. The games got tougher and they faced much more pressure.

They had their eye on the championship game. They knew if they were to make it they would have to face the strongest teams in college basketball. Each advance meant a tougher team and more pressure with the reward of a greater prize to the winner.

When David came out of the wilderness from watching his father's sheep, his first battle with the Philistines was against their best. Goliath was the biggest and the meanest of them all. When David stood on top of Goliath and cut off his head, the rest of the Philistine's fled. David easily handled their #1 soldier.

Jesus said that the gates of hell will not

prevail against the church, no matter what comes out of hell – even the devil himself. They will not defeat the church that is empowered by the Holy Ghost.

When the Shockers beat Gonzaga, I thought maybe Gonzaga just had a bad day. Then they beat La Sal, then Ohio State. I realized this was no fluke. After David defeated Goliath, he became the Captain of Saul's army. He was so successful that the women of Israel would come out and sing, "David has slain his ten thousands."
This was no fluke; he was a real giant slayer.

Chapter Seven
The One with the Anointing

Jesse had eight sons, but only one was able to stand on the battlefield against the giant. Why David? He was not the oldest or the biggest. He wasn't the strongest or even the wisest. So why him? What did he have that others did not have? Was it bravery or just plain guts? He was never trained in any type of military training. He was a shepherd boy. His life had consisted of taking care of his father's sheep and whatever it took to keep the family going. Most likely, since he was the youngest, he found himself doing those things that the others felt were dull and least important.

One thing we do recognize is that David had great faith. Is this what it takes to overthrow the enemy, great faith? Faith is essential for whatever we do for the Lord. But from where does the type of faith we see in David originate? Are we born with it or is it a certain style of schooling that we have to be raised under? If that is true, why did his brothers lack that type of faith since they grew up in the same home? Maybe it could be a gift from God to only certain people?

To comprehend the source of David's abilities we are only able to see what the writer gives us. The Bible tells us of the actions that started David's rise to be the prevailing king of Israel. The first physical glimpse of him is when he is summoned by Samuel to see if he is the one that God has hand-picked to be king. He is described as a very good looking young man. Nothing is said about his bodily strength. It is noted that Eliab was a mighty man so that when Samuel saw him, he thought surely he was the one God had chosen. Evidently, David did not possess a statuesque physique like his brother, Eliab.

Before David was presented with his brothers, God told Samuel that he had provided a king among Jesse's sons. David himself told King Saul of his encounter with the lion and the bear. David had already been chosen and trained by the Lord. I believe there has to be an amalgamation of factors to bring forth a person of David's caliber.

They must have the heart for the task at hand. David's brothers all passed before Samuel and none of them moved God. When David came and stood, God said, "This is he. Arise and anoint him." The Lord said that he had refused the others, Eliab, Abinadab, Shammah, Nethaneel, Raddai and Ozem, signifying that He must have considered each of them in turn and decided they did not have what it took.

If God was choosing a king based on loyalty, Samuel would be the one

Okay, David must have had a more courageous heart than his brothers. But what about Jonathan, Saul's son? He was clearly a godly and brave soldier. He was even next in line to be king since he was Saul's oldest son. I suppose there has to be more required to bring forth greatness than just being courageous.

Was that the key element that God was looking for loyalty? David was outraged at the words that Goliath had spoken against God and His army. He was loyal to the point he would go out and face a giant for his God. He was loyal to his father to watch over the sheep, even risking his life for them.

Well, what about the prophet Samuel? In all of Israel there was no one more loyal than he was. Why not Samuel? Why was he not chosen to be king? He had leadership abilities. He had led Israel to great victories over the Philistines. If God was choosing a leader based on loyalty, Samuel would have to be the man.

There had to be something else that God

saw in David that caused him to be chosen. We must remember that God was looking at the future of Israel, the big picture. A leader who would face incredible odds and not crack under the pressure of external or internal problems.

God and David had the same passion for Israel

To bring Israel to the forefront of kingdoms, there would be much opposition. God had a plan of victory for His people. However, finding someone to execute that plan is what he was looking for. God said, "I have found David the son of Jesse, a man after mine own heart, which shall fulfill all my will." This was the main key to David being selected by God over all of those in Israel.

Man after mine own heart! God and David had the same passion for Israel. God wanted to exalt his people to the forefront, that the entire world could see what it was like to be a nation that honored the real God. David, in his mind, saw Israel as the most honorable people in the world. He envisioned Israel as the beloved people of a great God.

That's why David was so disturbed by Goliath's cursing against Israel. David asked, "Who is this uncircumcised Philistine that he would defy the armies of the living God? Who is this unholy, unrighteous villain, mentally warped by the sin of fallen man that he would dare to speak against the Creator of all things and His chosen people?" This is not just some army of the kingdoms of fallen humanity, but the army of the living God.

God had instilled this type of courage, faith, and wisdom into David. It was a divine vision from heaven for God's people. That's why God said, "I have prepared me a king among Jesse's sons."

Jonathan was a courageous man. Also, he

was King Saul's oldest son, but it was never intended for him to be king over Israel. God's plan had not been implanted into the heart of Jonathan. He even knew himself that God had chosen David to be King. He told David in the wilderness that he would be king and he, Jonathan, would be next to him. Jonathan also gave him his robe, sword, and bow. He knew that day that David was the man to lead Israel. He did not have the vision for the kingdom. But he knew David did.

God instilled this into David's heart. The courage and faith David had been given had set him up for this task. Jacob had prophesied that the lawgiver would come from the tribe of Judah. Jonathan was from the tribe of Benjamin! Shiloh would be a descendant of Judah. God had already planned how things were going to come to pass.

Even before Jonathan and David were born, God had already spoken by the mouth of Jacob that from the tribe of Judah the lawgiver would come. Judah was Jacob's fourth son. Reuben was passed over because he had slept with his father's concubine. Simeon and Levi were disqualified when they killed innocent people over the incident with Shechem and their sister Dinah. Therefore the promise fell upon Judah.

I believe everyone has a God-called task and we are wired for that task. Deep inside we do have what it takes to fulfill the will of God for our lives. Not everyone is called to the same calling, responsibility or position. Jesus chose twelve disciples, but it is clear that Peter, James, and John were called to a more prominent role. They were given front row seats at the Mount of Transfiguration, the raising of Jared's daughter from the dead, and Jesus' prayer in the Garden of Gethsemane. Although they had a greater calling, in the end, with the exception of Judas, all the disciples accomplished much.

The more we fall in love with the body of Christ the more God uses us

This is a little hard for us to comprehend. It totally goes against our human nature that some are chosen by God and equipped by God to be more spiritually gifted than others in certain areas. This is also evident in nature. Bees have their drones, workers, and the queen. But it's not about them. It's about the survival of the hive. Clearly the queen bee is the most important in the colony. The drones and workers would quickly lay down their lives for her.

God places into the church those ministries that are needful to the edifying of the church. The more we fall in love with the body of Christ, the church, the more God uses us. This is the big picture. Jonathan was a great man. But he could see David as king and himself sitting next to him. David on the other hand saw Israel as the greatest nation in the whole world because of Almighty God and there was none like

Him.

David's agenda was for God and His nation to be exalted with no real thoughts on his own success. He really did not picture himself as king. He was shocked that Saul had asked him to marry his daughter. David saw his family as the least in Israel. His vision was not on himself or even his own kin, but on God and on Israel.

There are two requirements for the element of Greatness in your life – God and you! David was not the only person from the tribe of Judah and he was not the only son of Jesse. He was the one that had the faith and courage to benefit his God and the people of Israel. The faith of his brothers was lacking in that area. Mixing his faith with God's calling is what made David great.

We move forward as we conqueror.

We must have faith. But we also must walk in the plan that God has mapped out for our lives if we are going to reach the great potential He has destined for us. Some have zeal, but not according to the knowledge of God's purpose. Some know what God has called them to, but don't have the faith to step out.

Spending time alone with God is a must in order to learn to hear his voice. But then there comes a time when we must advance forward by faith in what God has revealed into our hearts. David said to King Saul that God had delivered him from the paw of the lion, the paw of the bear, and would deliver him out of the hand of the giant Philistine.

Knowing that the lion and the bear were delivered into his hands by God, he must have understood that there was a reason for this. He rehearsed this to King Saul on the battlefield. He was saying in essence, "God has already proved me and now I am ready for the task at hand."

We draw from our past victories to face the future trials

We move forward as we conquer. Victories over the lion and the bear spoke volumes about David's faith. The Lord had called him to be a protector, a deliverer, and a good steward of his father's sheep. That's the area where David carried the godly anointing. Every victory he experienced elevated him to a new level of confidence in God.

Our testimonies consist of God's great power to bring us through. We draw from our past victories to face the future trials. God brought me through then and He surely will bring me through now. Our faith is developed by the things we overcome. Our faith is weakened by the things that we allow to overcome us.

If David had not been able to save the lamb from the lion and he himself was badly injured, then when it came time to stand up against the giant, do you think he would have been able? I have seen believers with much zeal, but they did not have the spiritual knowledge of God's call for their lives. They jumped into an area that they were not called or anointed for and, after suffering much defeat, they limp away bound and broken in their faith. Some even felt that God had failed them.

We first have to know what direction we are to run

The three eldest brothers of David were also there that day. What if Shammah stepped up to fight the Philistine instead of David? Would the outcome have been the same?

It is imperative that we know God's will. If we are going to win the race we must run well. But we first have to know in which direction we are to run. To experience victory and a full life of faith and power, we must know who we are in the Lord.

On the day that David stood before Saul, he knew exactly who he was in God and what he was anointed for.

Then said David to the Philistine, "Thou comest to me with a sword, and with a spear, and with a shield: but I come to thee in the name of the LORD of hosts, the God of the armies of Israel, whom thou hast defied. This day will the LORD deliver thee into mine hand; and I will smite thee, and take thine head from thee; and I will give the carcasses of the host of the Philistines this day unto the fowls of the air, and to the wild beasts of the earth; that all the earth may know that there is a God in Israel. And all this assembly shall know that the LORD saveth not with sword and spear: for the battle is the LORD'S, and he will give you into our hands." (1 Sam 17:45-47 KJV)

David acknowledges that it was not his strength or skill that was going to win the battle, but the power of God that rested upon him for the victory. Are we anointed to win the battle against Satan? Jesus said that we are!

Luke 10:19 says, "Behold, I give unto you power to tread on serpents and scorpions, and over all the power of the enemy: and nothing shall by any means hurt you."

This was spoken to His disciples. As His followers, God has anointed us for the purpose of pulling down the enemies of His kingdom. Like David, the believers in Christ are called out and anointed with the oil of the Holy Ghost to slay the forces of the enemy. All Holy Ghost filled disciples of the Lord Jesus Christ have been empowered to pull down the strongholds of Satan.

"But ye shall receive power, after that the Holy Ghost is come upon you: and ye shall be witnesses unto me both in Jerusalem, and in all Judaea, and in Samaria, and unto the uttermost part of the earth." (Acts 1:8 KJV)

"And these signs shall follow them that believe; in my name shall they cast out devils; they shall speak with new tongues; they shall take up serpents; and if they drink any deadly thing, it shall not hurt them; they shall lay hands on the sick, and they shall recover." (Mark 16:17-18 KJV)

There are different callings in the body of Christ; not all are called to pastor, or to be prophets, but all filled believers have been anointed by the Holy Ghost to overpower the works of Satan.

If you have never received how can you give?

Jesus told the disciples to stay in Jerusalem until they were filled with the Holy Ghost. Paul questioned believers whether or not they had been filled with the Holy Ghost, yet Peter witnessed a Gentile group called together by Cornelius filled with Holy Ghost. It is clear that it is God's will that believers are to be full of His Spirit.

The first step of walking with power and victory is receiving the Holy Ghost. He said, "Freely you have received, freely give." If you have never received how can you give? If David was not anointed, he would have been just like his brothers. When Samuel poured the oil on David, the Spirit of the LORD came upon him from that day forward.

What is the anointing for? To break every yoke of bondage that Satan puts on us or others. We are called to be like David so that we may step out and face the forces that are coming against our churches, our families, and our own lives.

Chapter Eight
Royal Robe

"And Jonathan stripped himself of the robe that was upon him, and gave it to David, and his garments, even to his sword, and to his bow, and to his girdle." (1 Sam 18:4 KJV)

To give him his sword and his bow indicated that Jonathan wanted David to do his fighting for him. But I think he was most likely saying, "David you lead us." It is noted that in prior battles Saul and Jonathan were the only ones in Israel who had swords. Jonathan offered his weapons to David. There had to be something he saw in this young man to be willing to surrender his weapons to him.

When David went to the battle he had no sword. But, on that particular day, David received two swords, Jonathan's and Goliath the Philistine giant. One sword represented royalty and the other represented bravery. The sword of royalty was handed over to him by Jonathan, the king's son and heir to the throne. The other sword, the one of bravery, was won through victory on the battlefield. Royalty is a gift. Bravery has to be earned. But they must go together for the greatest success.

Royalty without bravery will become corrupt

After King Saul's death, his son Ish Bosheth took the throne. He was next in line after his father and brothers were killed in battle against the Philistines. He had royalty but not bravery. He could not even stand up to the captain of his own army. He was a weak leader ultimately betrayed and assassinated by his own men.

Ish Bosheth was given the throne but could not handle it. He was not chosen by God, but by man. To Abner, his father's uncle, the one who took Ish Bosheth and made him king, he seemed to be the right choice. Abner thought that, since he was Saul's only remaining son, Ish Bosheth should get the kingdom. This was a decision that Abner later regretted.

Royalty without bravery will become corrupt. Look at King Ahab. He did not have the guts to stand up for what was right. He allowed his wife, Jezebel, to rule his kingdom in an immoral way which resulted in his own demise.

As born again believers we are the children of the Most High God, walking in the power of the Holy Spirit to execute God's will.

"But ye are a chosen generation, a royal priesthood, an holy nation, a peculiar people; that ye should show forth the praises of him who hath called you out of darkness into his

marvelous light: Which in time past were not a people, but are now the people of God: which had not obtained mercy, but now have obtained mercy." (1 Pet 2:9-10 KJV)

We have royal blood in our veins

We have been called into the royal family of God. As kings and priests of the kingdom of heaven, we must defend it against the forces of darkness. We will be called upon on a daily basis to fight against seducing spirits and doctrines of devils.

We have been made sons and daughters of the Most High God by the royal blood of Jesus Christ. It is now up to us to be courageous for our Lord. Our job is to declare the gospel of the kingdom of righteousness to a lost world. We have royal blood in our veins. The kingdom is now our inheritance.

Are all believers called to walk in power?

The answer is yes! Do all believers walk in power? I believe we all know the answer to that question. Many have yet to tap into the power of God which He makes available through faith by the Holy Ghost.

At first glance it seemed David was just a shepherd boy, the youngest of his father's sons. He was just a young man called to play the harp for King Saul. The thought of him being kingly material was neither in the minds of his father nor his brothers. He was not even summoned to be presented before Samuel the prophet until Samuel requested that he be brought forth. Elab, his brother, scolded him when he spoke with authority against Goliath. Royalty was nowhere on the radar for young David.

From the tribe of Judah

Let's consider the roots of David. Was he royalty? He was handpicked by God, anointed by the prophet Samuel, and originated from the lineage of Judah. He was therefore a descendant of Boaz.

"And the women her neighbours gave it a name, saying, there is a son born to Naomi; and they called his name Obed: he is the father of Jesse, the father of David. Now these are the generations of Pharez: Pharez begat Hezron, And Hezron begat Ram, and Ram begat Amminadab, And Amminadab begat Nahshon, and Nahshon begat Salmon, And Salmon begat Boaz, and Boaz begat Obed, And Obed begat Jesse, and Jesse begat David." (Ruth 4:17-22 KJV)

David was of royal blood. He was a direct descendent of Abraham to whom the promise of the royal seed was given. He was also of the tribe of Judah out of which Jacob said the law-giver would come.

Therefore, when Jonathan offered over his royal possessions he was in reality giving them to the rightful heir of the throne. The promise came to Abraham because of his faith. It would only be right that David, by an act of faith, claimed it. In fact, that is how we all step into our royal position in Christ by faith.

Just maybe that's what Jonathan saw when David stepped out of the crowd to go up against the giant. In Jonathan's mind he may have thought, "Now there is a true son of Abraham a man of faith."

Sword of courage

Goliath's sword was later given to Ahimelech the priest. It was wrapped in an ephod and placed in the temple at Nob. David once again called upon it when he was fleeing from Saul. Although David was not afraid of the king, he did not want to bring division in Israel. David could have slain him on two occasions. But he refused to take Saul's life. David understood that God had placed Saul into the position as king and he was not going to fight against the will of God.

David's bravery brought him to opportunity to be presented as royalty. True royalty is obtained through bravery. You are not brave because you are of royalty. But you are royal because you are brave. Many are called, but few are chosen.

For the next several months David and his band of mighty men would persevere and exhibit many acts of bravery. They had been labeled as rebels and enemies of the crown by King Saul. They were cast out of the homeland and into the hostile territory of the Philistines.

When we are entering the realm of great opposition, God's word, the sword of the Spirit, will be made manifest to us with the power to overcome. Ahimelech the priest represented the Holy Ghost who had stored up the sword for such a time when it would be needed.

And the priest said, "The sword of Goliath the Philistine, whom thou slewest in the valley of Elah, behold, it is here wrapped in a cloth behind the ephod: if thou wilt take that, take it: for there is no other save that here."

And David said, "There is none like that; give it me." (1 Samuel 21:9 KJV)

The same faith in God's promises that brought you into this position is the same faith needed to carry you all the way through. The sword was laid up in the temple to be an example of God's ability to liberate Israel from their enemies.

Many today have done the same thing. They have taken the powerful Word of God along with all of the glorious testimonies of faithful deliverance and tucked them away in the house of God like a relic to be remembered once in a while.

David said to Ahimelech, "Give it to me." In other words, I need it now. That's what cut the head off the giant. It is still good for today. We like to sit around and speak in the past tense about the miracles of the Bible. The reality of God's Word is just as powerful today as it was then.

God's people handle with care

David was then a fugitive hunted by his own people by Saul's decree. He was also pursued as an enemy of the Philistines. He fled to the woods. Not in fear of the Philistines, but in fear of having to do battle with the children of Israel, his beloved countrymen.

We should never sidestep a battle with the devil. But we must use caution when an attack comes at us from within the ranks of the church. This will take bravery and wisdom. Yes, it was the spirit of jealousy that was moving the king to hunt after

David. But Saul was still God's chosen leader. We must not forget when the internal attacks come that it may be the hand of Satan at work. However, they are still God's people. Handle with care.

The plan of Satan is to divide and conquer. If we turn on each other we will weaken the body of Christ and that is exactly what he wants. The woods symbolize a solitary place. When warfare springs up in the body, we must seek a place of prayer and guidance from the Lord in order to keep things together. Our mouths can become weapons whereby we weaken or destroy one another. Stepping back and holding our peace until we have divine direction is a must. The enemy will push at us to unleash hurtful words upon each other. A godly person will refrain from speaking until he feels a release from the Spirit.

Give God time to work things out

Speaking as a pastor, when we are dealing with those within the church there are situations wherein we must act quickly to keep a firestorm from sweeping across the church. Then, there are those instances when you have to give God time to work things out. The end result will be that things are put in proper order so that God's will is fulfilled.

David had to flee from Saul. He positioned himself in a place of holding until things were worked out. I believe by this time David understood that he was to be king. He made it clear that if anything bad came upon King Saul, it would not be by his hand. He wanted his life and kingdom to be without guilt.

To those who are called into ministry there will be times when you will find yourself sitting where David sat. Let God elevate you and position you into the place of leadership. In the secular world it's a dog eat dog world. In the kingdom of God it's not so. His way is a road of humility. God wants to make you royalty. But you must stay humble and brave.

"Humble yourselves in the sight of the Lord, and he shall lift you up." (James 4:10 KJV)

When Jonathan gave David his robe, I wonder what King Saul thought when he looked upon David and saw his son's robe. He knew that Jonathan was next in line to be king and that must have been the king's desire. He even once warned Jonathan his son saying, "If David lives you will not be able to be king."

"For as long as the son of Jesse liveth upon the ground, thou shalt not be established, nor thy kingdom." (1 Sam 20:31 KJV)

It is clear to me that on the day Jonathan gave his robe to David he was relinquishing his claim to the throne. From that day forward he became a supporter in David's camp, even though it meant standing against his own father's will. Jonathan said of David's future,

"Fear not: for the hand of Saul my father shall not find thee; and thou shalt be king over Israel, and I shall be next unto thee; and that also Saul my father knoweth." *(1 Sam 23:17 KJV)*

I cannot think of a better person who would have made a good king other than Jonathan. He was courageous, wise, and caring. Evidently, he did not feel that he was called to be king. Not once did he ever mention his desire to be king or even hint about it. It seems he only wanted what was best for Israel. On the day that David stepped out to face the giant, Jonathan knew at that moment who would be the next leader of Israel.

As a new young pastor sitting in my first

church board meeting, I was very nervous. All of the deacons who sat at the table with me had been saved and faithfully following the Lord much longer than I had been saved. Their wisdom and knowledge of the Bible exceeded mine by far. They had great experience in keeping our church operating.

As pastor, I was also placed as the chairmen of this board. These men allowed me to lead the church and bark out orders. They submitted to this pastor who was wet behind the ears. Why would they do that? They loved the church. They had a loyal spirit and they believed in me.

Jonathan loved Israel. He was loyal even to his father who was doing wrong. He believed in what he saw in David. For those men to sit and allow this young pastor to preach to them displayed an aspect of greatness on their part. Truly, Jonathan had a great heart and a right spirit.

Chosen and equipped by God

The chemistry of spiritual royalty or godly leadership is made from several components. First and foremost, the individual has to have been chosen and equipped by God and wired for the purpose and tasks that the Spirit desires to accomplish through his life. This is not something we can just teach ourselves or be taught by others. It is gradually but firmly established in our spirit by God. Either you have it or you don't. This is what we are called to be by the will of God. He has put the desire to fulfill that calling into our hearts.

I am truly convinced that we are not satisfied until we finally step into the calling that God has ordained for us to walk in. Secular psychiatry even recognizes the need for fulfillment in the personal lives of individuals. Paraphrasing Ralph Waldo Emerson, Leo Rosten said, "The purpose of life is not to be happy – but to matter, to be productive, to be useful, and to have it make some difference that you have lived at all." (Rosen, 1965, p. 55)

Second comes personal searching and training to develop what God has placed into our hearts. Like gold in the ground it is there, although we must search to find it. There is also the process of bringing it to the surface where it may be processed for use. This is largely done by the assistance of the Holy Spirit. He, the Holy Spirit, leads us into all truths, trying us and bringing us into contact with others who have like gifts and callings.

Right time at the right place

Third comes timing – the right time at the right place. Moses tried to do the right thing at the wrong time when he stood up for the Israelite man who was beaten by an Egyptian guard. He knew God had called him to be a deliver for his people, but the tribes of Israel were not yet ready to be delivered. Our ministry has a time, a place, and a purpose.

"But when the fullness of the time was come, God sent forth his Son, made of a woman, made under the law," (Gal 4:4 KJV)

My wife and I felt led to go to Arkansas City, Kansas, to help a good friend of ours with his church. We became the associate pastors of the church. This position lasted for about two and half years. The church started going through some troubles. There were even times when I was pitted against my friends by others in the church. On several occasions, I prayed and asked God to release me and send me somewhere else. But the release never came.

One of the churches in our movement opened up and it was close to my friend's hometown so he took it. He stood on a

Sunday morning and said that next week would be his last week. Our whole reason for being there was to be a strength and support for him. Now that he was leaving I felt I had lost my purpose.

Every night that week I went to the church and prayed for direction for Diana and I. There was no guarantee that the new pastor would want an associate pastor. Would the new pastor desire to keep us on staff? Would I still have the same desire to work with someone different? These were the questions that came to mind.

I went to the church on a Wednesday afternoon to pray. The Lord spoke very clearly to me. He said, "This is why I brought you here. You will be the pastor of this church." I went straight home and told Diana I knew what we are supposed to do. Before I could tell her she said, "We are going to be the new pastors of the church." I said, "Yes, how did you know?" She said, "I was praying and the Lord told me that's what we were going to do."

The Lord led me to that church to be pastor, but the timing came later. He had positioned me there for that responsibility. Had I given into my feelings and left, I would have missed the timing for what God was doing in me and in the church. I have currently pastored that church for more than eighteen years.

Right person, Right purpose, Right time

Jonathan gave his royal robe to the right person for the right purpose at the right time. That's what I call a God moment, when everything comes together. Jonathan had no idea that the prophet Samuel had already anointed David to be the next king. He did not know anything about David's lineage or who he was.

It's so amazing how God is able to

orchestrate His will through us even when we don't have a clue what He is up to. God moves on our hearts and knits us together with His Spirit to perform His will.

This is exactly what God is planning for your life, that you will be the right person, in the right place, at the right time. This is flowing in the perfect will of God. When we hook up to the flow of His spirit, there will be many God orchestrated encounters.

Samuel put the oil on David's head. Jonathan put the robe on his back, and Ahimelech, the priest, put the sword in his hand. In our walk with God there will be many sent by God into our lives. These are not just coincidences. They have come by divine appointment.

God has purposefully placed us in a position to receive from them. Paul, the apostle, said to the believers at Rome, "For I long to see you, that I may impart unto you some spiritual gift, to the end ye may be established."

A covering of God's Holy Spirit

I believe it is God's desire for His people to wear a royal robe of power and righteousness. The first thing that Adam and Eve realized after they had sinned was that they were naked. They told God they hid from His voice because they were naked. He knew immediately that they had partaken of the forbidden fruit. Sin was not in their nature so He said, "Who told you that you were naked?"

They had a whole new mindset and outlook on things. No longer were they looking through the eyes of purity but through the eyes of sinful human desires. They quickly tried to cover their nakedness by going to the trees for leaves and sewed them together to make aprons as a covering.

God had given man the dominion. But he allowed Satan to deceive him into believing a lie. He was stripped of his human purity, righteousness, and authority. Because of his nakedness or insecurity, he began to seek a covering other than God's Holy Spirit.

Many today are not seeking the covering of God's Spirit but are eating the fruit of false religions and spirits of secular humanism, wearing the leaves of those teachings. They have justified their lifestyles by the covering of the things they believe. Evidently, God was not pleased with Adam and Eve's covering of leaves. He made them a covering that was more acceptable.

"Unto Adam also and to his wife did the LORD God make coats of skins, and clothed them." (Gen 3:21 KJV)

It is the will of God for His people to be clothed with glory and honor. That is something that can only come by His Spirit.

This world does not have a holy garment to cover our nakedness, our sin.

"Woe to the rebellious children, saith the Lord, that take counsel, but not of me; and that cover with a covering, but not of my spirit, that they may add sin to sin." (Isaiah 30:1 KJV)

God has a covering for us that is the Holy Ghost. This is why Christ came to give us His Spirit. It has been shed abroad for you and me, not a beggar's garment, but a royal robe with authority that comes from the Father.

God sent, or Satan sent

I also know that there are those whom Satan tries to place in our road to hinder us and load us down with things that are a threat or a burden to us. Saul wanted David to marry his daughter so that she would be a snare to him.

*"And Michal Saul's daughter loved David:
and they told Saul, and the thing pleased
him. And Saul said, I will give him her, that
she may be a snare to him, and that the
hand of the Philistines may be against him.
Wherefore Saul said to
David, Thou shalt this day be my son in law
in the one of the twain." (1 Samuel 18:20-21
KJV)*

It is pretty easy to tell if they are God sent
or Satan sent by the effect they have on us.
Are they pulling us down or lifting us up?
Are they a positive or a negative in our life?
Paul said he came to impart a spiritual gift.
Are they a gift in our life or a curse?

From the first time David met Jonathan, he
was blessed. I believe that the Lord placed
Jonathan into David's life as a type of priest.
Just as the priest of old would anoint and
crown the new kings, Jonathan placed his
royal robe on David. The priest would go

before the Lord to intercede for the king. Jonathan interceded to his father on David's behalf. The priests as spiritual leaders would give prophetic counsel to the king. Jonathan foretold to David that he would one day sit as king of Israel.

David did not steal the kingdom from Saul. It was given to him by God and endorsed by Jonathan, the rightful heir of King Saul. We must not allow ourselves to impose upon someone else's possessions. If something is meant for us, we don't have to take it by force. God will give it to us.

"Every good gift and every perfect gift is from above, and cometh down from the Father of lights, with whom is no variableness, neither shadow of turning." *(James 1:17 KJV)*

Chapter Nine
Eyes of Saul

"And it came to pass as they came, when David was returned from the slaughter of the Philistine, that the women came out of all cities of Israel, singing and dancing, to meet King Saul, with tabrets, with joy, and with instruments of music. And the women answered one another as they played, and said, Saul hath slain his thousands, and David his ten thousands. And Saul was very wroth, and the saying displeased him; and he said, "They have ascribed unto David ten thousands, and to me they have ascribed but thousands: and what can he have more but the kingdom?" And Saul eyed David from that day and forward." (1 Sam 18:6-9 KJV)

David was no longer a hero in Saul's eyes. He was a threat to his position as king. It was now clear to Saul that the people of Israel esteemed David more highly than they esteemed him. Saul was the king. Yes! He had royalty, but he did not have bravery.

Saul's insecurities and fears were now coming to the surface. He was not brave enough to go out before the giant. Someone else had fight the battle for him. He then feared that he would not be able to hold on to the kingdom.

It is apparent that somewhere in the past he lost his faith in God's sustaining ability. David, on the other hand, told Saul that the God who saved him from the paw of the lion and the bear would deliver him from the uncircumcised Philistine. He was confident in God's ability to safeguard him and help him prevail against the giant.

Insecure people become the greatest obstacles to the work of God

Saul no longer had the faith that it took to

be a mighty king. It is possible that he never had that much confidence in Almighty God's power in the first place. His faith did rise on some occasions. But on several occasions he did not fully obey the voice of the Lord.

There was much self-doubt in Saul. He second guessed both his decisions and the Lord's commands. He had not entirely sold out and given everything to God. Coincidentally, he could not fully place his trust in the Lord.

Insecure people become hindrances in the body of Christ. They will chase away anyone they feel is a threat to their position and authority. They seize control and hang on to it as if their lives depend on it. Because of their weak faith, they have trouble trusting God to lift them up and keep them in that position.

They will try to take things by force and

keep them by any means necessary. They don't give God opportunity to work things out for the good. They become instruments of sabotage to the work that the Lord is doing. They are being led of their own will and not the will of God.

When my daughter Angel was about four years old we had a yard sale to get rid of some stuff that was good but no longer needed. We went through Angel's toy box. She had a lot of things that she had outgrown or did not play with anymore – or so we thought.

On the day of the sale we put everything out on the tables in the front yard. Throughout the day I noticed Angel coming in and out of the house. As I watched her she would go to the tables, find her old toys, and take them back into the house. She did not want to give them up.

As we grow we must learn to change. That

means letting go of some things so that we may move on to greater things. If we hold on to those things of the past and are unwilling to let go, we cannot move on to the next level of our lives.

Diana and I understood that Angel was moving from being a toddler to becoming a child. She still had a connection in her heart for those things, even if they were beneath her emerging new abilities. Our lives are a constant changing process not easily adjusted. If we are not willing to change, we find ourselves holding on to things even when it is time to let go.

It was time for Saul to let go, but he would not. He hardened his heart against God and stiffened his neck. Saul's fears hindered his good judgment toward the work of God.

He became jealous toward the one that God was raising up. He felt that he was pushed to the side. He started working behind the scenes to undermine anyone considered to be a threat to him.

I have observed this same spirit operating in the body of Christ today. It comes from those who have allowed their spirits to become cold and disconnected. They give in to the old man of fear, jealousy, and strife.

David fully trusted in his God

When David's son Absalom deceitfully rose to power, King David did not try to have him executed or imprisoned, not even when he tried to take the kingdom by force. Instead of fighting, David ran. He knew that God was able to keep him and bring him back.

"And the king said unto Zadok, Carry back the ark of God into the city: if I shall find favour in the eyes of the LORD, he will bring me again, and show me both it, and his

habitation: But if he thus say, I have no delight in thee; behold, here am I, let him do to me as seemeth good unto him." (2 Sam 15:25-26 KJV)

David fully trusted in his God! He knew that his life belonged to the Lord and he totally relied upon the will of God in his life. All that he was and all that he had been was because of his God. He let God make the choice between him and Absalom as to who should be king in Israel just as he let God choose between him and Saul.

There will always be a conflict when jealousy is present

It did not take long for trouble to erupt between David and Saul. There will always be a conflict when jealousy is present. It's hard to get along with someone who despises you. Saul's jealousy turned into murderous hatred. He at one time loved David greatly and had even made him his armour bearer.

Saul then felt threatened by David's success. He felt that David had stolen the hearts of the people away from him. He was once the hero of Israel. Then it seemed that he was only second best. You may have watched the classic movie Toy Story when the boy, Andy, got a new toy, Buzz Lightyear. Woody, the cowboy, was Andy's favorite toy until Buzz came along. Now, Woody had to stay in the toy box with the other toys while Buzz slept on the bed with Andy. That was the place Woody used to sleep.

Woody perceived if he could just get rid of Buzz he would be back in his place as Andy's favorite toy. This was the same thinking with Saul. He knew he was losing his position as the favorite son of Israel and being replaced as number one in the eyes of the people. Also, laying in the back of his mind were the words of Samuel who told him that the Lord was going to take the kingdom of Israel from him and give it to a neighbor who was better than him.

It is clear that all this was eating at Saul's mind and spirit. He could no longer speak peaceably to David. Saul knew that he had lost his place with God and subsequently with the people. He saw that the people loved David and that the hand of God rested upon him. He allowed fear to set in his heart that David was going to take his place.

There are rules to fighting in the Spirit! If we are going to win this battle, we must engage with pureness of heart. I understand in the world that you can't be a gentleman in a fight. But fighting in the Spirit is much different. You cannot use the weapons or the tactics of the enemy. If you do, he wins.

Satan's weapons are hatred, jealousy, strife and so on. If we use these weapons to fight those who are coming against us, the battle is over. Instead of defeating the works of the enemy, we become a part of them.

David understood this. He did not give into those spirits when he was chased by Saul and by his own son, Absalom. He allowed God to overthrow his enemies. There are different ways of handling spiritual warfare. It depends on who you are fighting. Are they fellow Israelites or Philistines?

"And Saul was afraid of David, because the LORD was with him, and was departed from Saul." (1 Sam 18:12 KJV)

Saul was troubled by an evil spirit. His heart was not right with God. This is the place where Satan can take control. Fear and jealousy does not come from God. Allowing this into his heart warped his good judgment. Saul became obsessed with destroying the very person that brought victory to Israel over the giant and the army of the Philistines.

"And it came to pass on the morrow, that the evil spirit from God came upon Saul, and he prophesied in the midst of the house: and David played with his hand, as at other times: and there was a javelin in Saul's hand. And Saul cast the javelin; for he said, I will smite David even to the wall with it. And David avoided out of his presence twice." (1 Sam 18:10-11 KJV)

David was actually the most faithful friend that Saul had

What did David do to Saul to cause him to hate him to the point of plotting his murder? Nothing! Now let's look at what did David do for Saul? He played the harp for him until the evil spirit left, he carried his armor, and he defeated the giant that came against Saul's army. He also lead Saul's troops to great victories over the Philistines. David became a good friend to

Saul's son, Jonathan, married and took care of Saul's daughter, Michal. He did not allow any of his men to harm Saul when they could have easily taken his life. Even after Saul's death, David executed the man who said that he had slain King Saul and had the two captains who betrayed and slew Saul's son Ish Bosheth executed.

Wow! David was actually the most faithful friend that Saul had. No one stood up for Saul like David did. But yet Saul hated him. If we allow it, jealousy and fear have the power to harden our hearts, blind our eyes, and turn us against those who are trying to help us.

It is the desire of demonic spirits to completely control a person's life. They come in to take over. They are not satisfied with just a little control. Saul's suspicions began to take on new depths. He had seventy of God's priests killed because he thought they were trying to help David behind his back. He even accused Jonathan of taking David's side and cast a spear at his own son.

Evil spirits want to be in complete control

"Then Saul's anger was kindled against Jonathan, and he said unto him, Thou son of the perverse rebellious woman, do not I know that thou hast chosen the son of Jesse to thine own confusion, and unto the confusion of thy mother's nakedness? For as long as the son of Jesse liveth upon the ground, thou shalt not be established, nor thy kingdom. Wherefore now send and fetch him unto me, for he shall surely die, and Jonathan answered Saul his father, and said unto him, Wherefore shall he be slain? What hath he done? And Saul cast a javelin at him to smite him: whereby Jonathan knew that it was determined of his father to slay David. So Jonathan arose from the table in fierce anger, and did eat no meat the second day of the

month: for he was grieved for David, because his father had done him shame." (1 Sam 20:30-34 KJV)

Saul had become obsessed with destroying David to the extent that nothing else mattered to him. He came to the realization that David was the one of whom Samuel had spoken. God was going to take the kingdom from Saul and give it to a neighbor.

"And he said to David, Thou art more righteous than I: for thou hast rewarded me good, whereas I have rewarded thee evil. And thou hast showed this day how that thou hast dealt well with me: forasmuch as when the LORD had delivered me into thine hand, thou killest me not. For if a man find his enemy, will he let him go well away? wherefore the LORD reward thee good for that thou hast done unto me this day. And now, behold, I know well that thou shalt surely be king, and that the kingdom of Israel

shall be established in thine hand." (1 Sam 24:17-20 KJV)

Saul verbally acknowledged that David would one day be king. Then, when he heard that David was in a certain place, he gathered his army and pursued him again. Wow! What mixed feelings! What confusion! He knew that it was God's will for David to be king. Why didn't Saul just bow out and say, "Here David. You take the kingdom?"

He may not have maintained his position as king. But at least he would have saved his life and the lives of his sons. Saul's eyes were blinded by his own pride and jealousy. He was not able to make good choices for the well-being of himself, his family, or the kingdom.

When we turn our back on God, our hearts become hardened. Unless we have a true act of repentance and humbly turn back to

Him, we are doomed. Our hardened hearts cannot be detoured by human reasoning. The nation of Israel experienced this very act. They turn from following God unto idols. He sent His Word to them by holy men, but the people stiffened their necks to his Word.

What happened to Saul could have happened to anyone of us. Our obedience to God means the difference in working with Him or working against Him. I know that down through the ages there have been great onslaughts against the body of Christ. The greatest battles to plague the church are not those that come from without the church, but those that come from within.

When we as a people become relaxed in our faith, sit back, and quit fighting, we open our hearts to every evil spirit to come in and use us to hurt the brothers in Christ. We will never forget what took place on

911 when terrorists boarded our own planes, took control, and used them to kill American citizens. That is exactly how Satan infiltrates the church. He works though the children of disobedience.

As believers we expect persecution from the unbelievers in the world. The United States was prepared for attack with all kinds of weapons to protect the borders. We were prepared to shoot down long range missiles. However, we were not prepared for 911 because the threat, the vicious attack, came from within.

Most believers suffer injury and hurt from within the ranks of the church by those who call themselves Christians yet have not crucified the flesh. Such injurious parties are walking in disobedience to the voice of God just as King Saul did.

On 911, the US Air force did not shoot any planes down even though they came close to it. The planes were friendly planes with innocents as well as hostiles aboard. That created quite a dilemma.

The spiritual battle that we fight must be bathed in prayer and directed by the Holy Ghost with our will submitted in obedience to God. There are hostiles out there. But there are also friendlies in the mix. We cannot just sit around and let missiles fly out of our mouths when we feel we're under an attack.

Life and death are in the power of the tongue. We have the ability to build up or tear down. God has called us to lift up the body of Christ and put the works of Satan under our feet.

Chapter Ten
As King

And it came to pass after this that David inquired of the LORD, saying, "Shall I go up into any of the cities of Judah?"
And the LORD said unto him, "Go up."
And David said, "Whither shall I go up?"
And he said, "Unto Hebron." (2 Samuel 2:1 KJV)

David did not take it for granted that Israel was his for the taking once Saul was dead. He consulted the Lord, asking Him if he should even return and enter into Israel. You would think that he would have assembled his men and gone straight up to secure the kingdom under his hand.

It is clear that he had no thirst for power or position. He wanted God's approval and direction for his future steps. A hostile takeover would only divide Israel. There are things that we can make happen and there are things that we must let God bring to pass.

David spent the next seven years in Hebron ruling over the tribe of Judah. He was given a portion of the kingdom but not the entire kingdom. There is a perfect timing for everything God ordains. Not all the people of Israel were ready to accept David as king. There were those who were still loyal to the former monarchy of Saul.

Many times we see this take place in the church world. God makes changes, but there are those who hold onto the former traditions. Saul's reign was good for its time. But God was taking Israel to a level they would never have been able to reach under Saul's leadership.

David wanted to be king only by God's approval and the consent of the people. He did not want to thrust himself into that position. He continued on with God's plan knowing that if God desired him as king He would make a way for him. Contemporary Christian artist Bryan Duncan sings a song entitled *Love Takes Time*. Well, that can also be said about God's plans. They take time and we must allow God to fulfill His will in His time. God's appointed time is always the appropriate time.

We can learn it the hard way or we can learn it God's way

Thinking back on the first church that I pastored, I don't believe I was ready to pastor a church at that time. I was twenty-three years old and had no clue what I was getting into. I was raised a pastor's son. I saw how my dad handled things and how they went, or so I thought. Evidently, there were many things that my folks dealt with behind the scenes of which I had no clue. I feel so sorry for those poor people at my first church that had to put up with this wet-behind-the-ears kid trying to be a preacher. I remember one time when I rode up on my ten speed bike to a couple of ladies. One of them attended my church. She looked at the other one and pointed at me and said, "This is our pastor," in a repugnant voice. Both of them were probably old enough to be my grandmother. I have to admit I did not look like your typical man of the cloth.

Of one thing I had no doubts. God had called me into the ministry. He really did a number on me because pastoring was definitely not on the top of my list. Actually, I don't think it was on my list at all until God put it there.

Pastoring this church was me jumping out before God was ready for me to go. I learned a lot. But I had to learn it the hard way. If I would have waited for the Lord to open the door when I was ready, things would have been much easier. We can learn it the hard way or we can learn it God's way.

The carnal mind cannot perceive the work of the Holy Spirit

Abner, Saul's uncle and captain of Saul's army, took Ish Bosheth, the son of Saul, and set him up as king over Israel. Yet, David was the king chosen by God from the time that Samuel poured oil upon his head in the midst of his brothers.

What Abner saw as right was due to the wisdom and understanding of carnal man, doing what seems right at the time. But the spirit that is in man cannot comprehend the work of the Holy Spirit. Remember, when Saul had asked him who the young man was that just defeated the giant, Abner could not tell that it was David. He did not recognize him even though David had been Saul's armor bearer. Neither Saul nor Abner had any clue who David was on that day. The carnal mind cannot perceive the work of the Holy Spirit or those who are being used by God.

One thing I have noticed taking root in the church world today is carnality. So many have cast off what God's Word says and have interjected their own rationality.

As a believer I have been shocked by the number of those who call themselves God's people but do not obey or even believe what the Scriptures say. People are living lifestyles that are clearly condemned by God's Holy Word. They have relied upon their own reasoning to justify and live a lifestyle that is contrary to the Word of God.

God is wiser than we are!

To be born again means to die to one's self and be resurrected by the power of Jesus

Christ.

"What? Know ye not that your body is the temple of the Holy Ghost which is in you, which ye have of God, and ye are not your own? For ye are bought with a price: therefore glorify God in your body, and in your spirit, which are God's." (1 Cor 6:19-20 KJV)

I cannot just accept Him as the atonement for my sins. I must make Him the Lord over every area of my life. Jesus Christ is the Word of God according to St John 1:1. I must trust in His Word, knowing that it is truth. Everything the Word of God declares about being saved has come to pass in my life. Everything that the Word proclaims about the power of the Holy Ghost and the gifts of the Spirit are operating in my life as truth.

I have not just read the Word of God. I have experienced it. I know it is right because it works. So, if it is truth, then I must yield my reasoning, thoughts, feelings, and passions to the true Word of God, no matter what I think or feel to the contrary.

God is wiser than we are! What He has said is to help prevent us from warping our minds and destroying our souls. If we allow pride to puff up our flesh and we snub our noses at His Word that will set events in motion that will bring harm and pain to our spirits and our lives.

Not all knowledge is good for us

When Eve looked at the tree of knowledge of good and evil she saw that it was good for food. She could not see the spiritual damage that would take place by exposing her mind and soul to the elements of sin. God knew this and that's why he told them, "You can eat of every tree in the garden except the tree of knowledge of good and evil."

To reject God's counsel in our hearts sets in motion the carnality of man. The Bible says that carnality is enmity or hostility toward God. The Creator of our mind, soul, and body knows exactly what will keep us functioning in a spiritually healthy condition.

Many live empty and unfulfilled lives because they have rejected God's Word and prevented it from reigning over their hearts and minds. Some seek for an act of repentance to remove the weight of sin's guilt off of them, but they do not surrender completely and allow Him to be the Lord of their life.

Setting up Ish Bosheth as king proved to be Abner's downfall

Abner was not able to protect Saul, the king, from intruders when they lay in the trenches. Likewise, the carnal man cannot keep us from spiritual attacks. Carnality is the reasoning that comes from the fallen nature of this world. It perceives not the working of the Spirit.

"And David said to Abner, Art not thou a valiant man? And who is like to thee in Israel? Wherefore then hast thou not kept thy Lord the king? For there came one of the people in to destroy the king thy Lord." (1 Sam 26:15 KJV)

People who operate in the carnal realm are those who lean to their own reasoning rather than seeking the will of God in a situation. They find themselves missing the will of God, unprotected against the spiritual elements, and vulnerable to confusion.

"For we wrestle not against flesh and blood, but against principalities, against powers, against the rulers of the darkness of this world, against spiritual wickedness in high places." (Eph 6:12 KJV)

Setting up Ish Bosheth as king proved to be Abner's downfall. He was not willing to accept David's rule as king. Using Saul's youngest son as a puppet king, since Abner knew that the people would reject him as king, Abner tried to usurp God's ordained authority. Though Ish Bosheth had clearly been of age to fight with his father and brothers against the Philistines, for some reason he had never done so.

Ish Bosheth did not stake claim to the throne until Abner seduced him into that position. He was a king in the flesh, but not in the Spirit. He had position, but he did not have courage. He could not even stand up to his own captains. Abner, the one who set him up to be king, did not even respect his position or fear him as king. He went in and lay with King Saul's concubine with no fear of what Ish Bosheth the new king would think of his treason.

Our own reasoning will betray us. It twists

things to fulfill the desire of the flesh. Abner only used Ish Bosheth. The carnal man works through the weakness of the flesh.

In the end, Abner and Ish Bosheth turned against each other over Rizpah, Saul's concubine. When Ish Bosheth tried to stand up to Abner, their relationship went south. Our reasoning can easily overpower our flesh. If there is something that you know you're not supposed to do, but you sit and cogitate about it long enough, you will find yourself doing it. Our reasoning can easily subdue our weak flesh.

Abner's death was at the hands of Joab and Abishai to avenge the killing of their brother Asahel. Ish Bosheth was beheaded by two of his own captains. Ironically, his head was buried in the tomb with the one who had set him up as king. In the Bible, the head represents authority. Abner was laid to rest with the head of the one he deceitfully put in position as king.

When Saul's son heard that Abner was dead, his hands were feeble. He had trusted in Abner to establish his kingdom. Now that he was dead, Ish Bosheth had no power to stand.

We all at one time had mouths that were bigger than our brains

Many are standing on their own knowledge and carnal reasoning. They will look at those they call people-of-faith and say that is only a crutch for the weak minded. Their pride has blinded their own eyes. I have noticed that most of these individuals are younger adults who, being so inexperienced, have not yet reached a place where their wisdom and knowledge was unable to pull them out of a crisis.

Recently I have been reconnected by Facebook to many of my old school friends. I have often wondered about their spirituality because many of them were not living for God or even acknowledge Him when we were in school. To my delight, the ones that I have come in contact with all have strong faith and are very verbal about it.

Like me, they have lived long enough to realize that although their abilities are limited, God's power is unlimited. We all at one time had mouths that were bigger than our brains.

David did not trust in his own reasoning or in the words of others. He sought the Lord for confirmation of his rise to the throne. He knew that he would not be able to place himself in that position. He also knew if he was placed by a man, like Ish Bosheth, it would not last.

"And David perceived that the Lord had established him king over Israel, and that he had exalted his kingdom for his people

Israel's sake." (2 Samuel 5:12)

Why was David placed into the position as King? For the people of Israel! All this was not for David, but for God's people. God had established a man as king who would fulfill His will and that man was David.

Before we get a big head because of our promotion, we must first ask ourselves why we are being promoted. The ones who gave us the promotion did not give it to us for our self-gratification. They placed us there because they believed we could accomplish the task.

That is what promotion is all about, the ability to do the job. During one of our church elections a member ran for one of the deacon positions. He was not elected! Evidently that upset him greatly, so much so that he left the church. I thought to myself he should have been overjoyed that he did not get that position. You have to listen to all the complaints, make hard decisions, and have people turn against you, all for no pay. He wanted the prestige of the position. Many look at position as a glory to their reputation and social status. But they don't look at the responsibility which is what a leadership position is all about.

President. When we hear that title we think authority, power, and a great position. Yes, it is all that. But it also comes with tremendous responsibilities. So much so that most men that have held that office age extremely fast in the short time they are there.

David never once said that he wanted to be king. Many others said to him that God was going to establish his kingdom. There was a man that witnessed Saul and his sons die in battle. He took Saul's crown and brought it to David supposing that was what David wanted as though David would be overjoyed to have it.

David did not force or advance himself into the position as king. He left that responsibility totally to God. David's main focus was just being obedient to the Lord. Jesus confirmed this type of thinking in the gospel of Matthew.

"But seek ye first the kingdom of God, and his righteousness; and all these things shall be added unto you." (Matt. 6:33 KJV)

Fleshly sins and spiritual sins

David's reign as king also had controversy. His sin with the wife of Uriah the Hittite and numbering the people to see how powerful his forces were things which angered the Lord.

The difference between Saul's sins and David's sins was that Saul's were out of rebellion and David's was from weakness of the flesh. You could say Saul's were spiritual sins and David's were fleshly sins.

I know sin is sin. But there is a difference when you do something out of direct disobedience. Let's look at it this way. Two men in a certain honorable king's kingdom are brought before the king for crimes they have committed. The first is charged with stealing and eating someone's chicken. The King sentences him to two days in the slammer and to repay the owner the cost of the chicken.

The second man is charged with telling the people they don't have to obey the king. The king sentences him to the guillotine to have his head chopped off. The man who lost his head stole nothing. He did not kill anyone but his punishment was much more severe than the thief's punishment.

It is easy to understand what the king perceived and why he made his verdict. One was stealing to satisfy his hunger while the other man committed high treason against the king. If that man was allowed to continue, the authority of the king and eventually the kingdom would fall.

Saul's sin was a direct attack on God's sovereignty and it influenced Israel, the people of God. If Saul were allowed to continue in the direction in which he had turned, he would have quickly become a tyrant instead of a good king. In fact, that is what he was before his death, trying to kill innocent people.

This is a common situation we all face because of the unconverted self-centered heart. This takes place in church and also in business or any place where there is position and power. It comes down to the motives of the heart. Why would this man try to turn the people against the king? Was it that he did not like the way things were being done? Did he want to be king himself? Maybe he did not want to submit to any type of authority.

Rebellion is a sin that opens the door of

our spirit for demonic control. When Saul refused to obey the voice of the Lord concerning the Amalekites, Samuel told him;

"For rebellion is as the sin of witchcraft, and stubbornness is as iniquity and idolatry. Because thou hast rejected the word of the Lord, he hath also rejected thee from being king." (1 Samuel 15:23 KJV)

God is merciful and is willing to pardon our transgressions. As the Psalmist says, God is slow to anger. But he will not allow demonic spirits to rule over His people. If we become a vessel that is used by Satan to influence the people of God, we will find ourselves crashing upon the rocks and sinking into despair.

King Ahab, a king of Israel, allowed his wife Jezebel to influence his life and the people of Israel with her witchcraft. She even went as far as setting up prophets of a false God to be worshiped. The end result was that Ahab and even his offspring were cut off and cursed by God.

Leadership in the body of Christ means everything. Without good godly leaders, darkness and confusion set in to divide and conquer. To follow the Holy Spirit is a must. It is said that George Washington once said, "It is impossible to rightly govern a nation without God and the Bible."

This was the example that David, the king, held to throughout his reign. Before battles he would ask the priests, Zadok, the son of Ahitub, and Ahimelech, the son of Abiathar, to seek instructions from the Lord for his guidance. Nathan and Gad were his closest advisers, prophets who revealed God's plans to him.

We have a High Priest named Jesus Christ making intersection on our behalf. He has given of His Spirit, the Holy Ghost, to lead us into all truths. The Bible, which is His living Word, is given to us for instructions, wisdom to understand God's ways, knowledge of how to build up the body of Christ - the church, and understanding of the spiritual realm.

No matter what area of leadership or ministry you are called to, God has already provided for you. It is His desire for you to be the best of the best at what He has called you to. We all have insecurities and flaws which is why we must follow the leading of His Spirit.

David became a great king, because he understood where his help came from. It was not his wisdom or strength, but the Lord's.

"According as his divine power hath given unto us all things that pertain unto life and godliness, through the knowledge of him that hath called us to glory and virtue:" (2 Peter

1:3)

Epilogue

"The hand of the LORD was upon me, and carried me out in the spirit of the LORD, and set me down in the midst of the valley which was full of bones, and caused me to pass by them round about: and, behold, there were very many in the open valley; and, lo, they were very dry. And he said unto me, Son of man, can these bones live? And I answered, O Lord GOD, thou knowest. Again he said unto me, Prophesy upon these bones, and say unto them, O ye dry bones, hear the word of the LORD. Thus saith the Lord GOD unto these bones; Behold, I will cause breath to enter into you, and ye shall live: And I will lay sinews upon you, and will bring up flesh upon you, and cover you with skin, and put breath in you, and ye shall live; and ye shall know that I am the LORD. So I prophesied as I was commanded: and as I prophesied, there was a noise, and behold a shaking, and the bones came together, bone to his bone. And when I beheld, lo, the sinews and the flesh came up *upon them, and the skin covered them above: but there was no breath in them. Then said he unto me, Prophesy unto the wind, prophesy, son of man, and say to the wind, Thus saith the Lord GOD; Come from the four winds, O breath, and breathe upon these slain, that they may live. So I prophesied as he commanded me, and the breath came into them, and they lived, and stood up upon their feet, an exceeding great army. Then he said unto me, Son of man, these bones are the whole house of Israel: behold, they say, Our bones are dried, and our hope is lost: we are cut off for our parts. Therefore prophesy and say unto them, Thus saith the Lord GOD; Behold, O my people, I will open your graves, and cause you to come up out of your graves, and bring you into the land of Israel. And ye shall know that I am the LORD, when I have opened your graves, O my people, and brought you up out of your graves, And shall put my spirit in you, and ye shall live, and I shall place you in your own land: then shall ye know that I the LORD have spoken it, and performed it, saith the LORD."*

(Ezekiel 37:1-14 KJV)

Like Ezekiel, Samuel, and many other God-called prophets of the Old Testament, there are also chosen men and women today and God is speaking into their hearts to prophesy to this generation. They may seem spiritually dry and disconnected, but by the Spirit of the living God they will come together.

When Samuel came to Bethlehem, David was only a young shepherd boy. David met the king anointer that day and the power of the Holy Spirit came upon him from that day forward. David knew that he was changed. He stood before Goliath with no fear in him at all.

At this time, God is raising up an army that will stand in the very face of demonic principalities with no fear or doubt. They will be committed to their God and His kingdom. They will not falter in the midst of the battle.

Let all of the Samuel's and Ezekiel's come forth today with an anointed word that will revive the hearts and spirit of this generation. There are Davids, Johnathans, Elishas, Peters, Pauls, Timothys and many more waiting for Samuels, king anointers, to arrive in Bethlehem today and pour the anointing upon them.

Church, this is our time to move forward. God has already prepared those who are to stand in this last hour. Today we find Goliaths taunting the church and Sauls who have become disconnected from the leading of the Holy Ghost.

Nebuchadnezzar had a dream of a great statue that had a head of gold, arms of silver, thighs of brass, legs of iron, and feet of iron mixed with clay. Daniel told Nebuchadnezzar that the statue represented the kingdoms of the world that would rise up to rule over Israel. At the end of his dream he saw a stone that smote the statue in the feet and caused it to crumble. Then the stone became a great mountain.

The kingdoms of this world will come to an end. The kingdom of Christ is the stone. The feet represented the last kingdom which will be that of the Antichrist. All these kingdoms will come to an end. The only one that will remain will be the Kingdom of our Lord Jesus Christ. This is what it is all about. Either we are with Him or we are against Him. We must choose which kingdom we are going to be a part of. I hope that you choose the kingdom that will last for all eternity.

Glossary

Meaning of words in the content of this book:

King Anointer: Someone who has been entrusted to call out and commission those whom God has chosen.

Spiritual Coach: Someone who has knowledge and understanding of how the Spirit of God operates and in which direction the Spirit is moving. They have been established by God to convey this spiritual wisdom and direction to us.

Man-Led Kingdom: A society that has chosen its own desires and reasoning to lead rather than yielding to the truths of the Holy Bible, God's Word, and allowing the Holy Spirit to guide them.

God-Led Kingdom: A society allowing

the Holy Spirit to direct life in every area in business, marriage, family, and government, believing that all things will be fulfilled promised in God's Word. The supernatural work of God is operating through the lives of those beneficiaries living under the spiritual authority, grace, and favor of such a society.

Kingdom of Darkness: The spiritual community of rebellious angels led by Satan that tried to exalt themselves above God. They have become a realm of twisted and perverted spirits that, under the leadership of Satan, try to usurp authority from the children of God.

Carnal Man: The human mind, the mind that leans upon reasoning that appeals to the lust and desires of the flesh rather than work of the Holy Spirit.

Spiritual Man: One who has truly been born-again so that the spirit has come alive on the inside so that the mind has been renewed by the Spirit of the living God. They do not yield to their own carnal thoughts, but to the preeminent authority of God's Word.

Church: Lighthouse of truth and Godly instructions shining into a lost and dark world.

Stuff: Things that we have connected our hearts to that only hinder us from fully obeying the will of God for our lives.

Sheep: Those who have a willing spirit and desire to be led by the Spirit of God.

Mules: Those who are self-willed, choosing to go their own way rather than yielding to the authority and direction of the Spirit of God.

God Encounter: A life changing event with the realm of the supernatural that is divinely appointed by God.

Seer: A prophet of the Lord that was able to see future events.

Blueprint of His will: Foreordained plans that God has laid out for us and the body of Christ so all things will work together for His divine purpose.

New Oil: A fresh outpouring of the Holy Ghost for a new upcoming generation.

Uncircumcised: Led by the desire of the flesh with no godly respect or discipline.

Flock: A group of God's people.

Lion: A furious demonic spirit that attacks the people of God through a verbal assault.

Bear: Stubborn territorial demonic spirit that maims anything that it feels is a threat to it.

Wolves: Demonic spirits that stalk the young, weak, and unprotected.

Keeper: One who has or has been entrusted with something of great value.

Searcher: One who has not and desires to have, or, someone who lost what they had previously and is now seeking it again.

Shepherd: A person set up by God to watch over the spiritual well-being of His people.

Good-Shepherd: Jesus. (John 10:11-14)

Hireling: Person that is acting as a shepherd, but has no real love or investment in the sheep. (John 10:12-13)

Giant: A demonic principality.

Sword: Weapon of great spiritual power. (Ephesians 6:17)

Stone: God's solid Word of deliverance.

Anointing: The power of the Holy Ghost resting upon us to destroy the forces of darkness that oppose God's people. (Isaiah 10:27)

Royal Robe: Spiritual covering of God's righteousness and authority.

Covering: The spiritual code of life that we have chosen to live by.

Nakedness: Sin and guilt exposed.

Beggars Garment: An ungodly spiritual covering lacking the protection, faith, and power necessary in order to, by the Holy Spirit, gracefully receive the benefits of the kingdom of God.

The End

References:

1. Basler, Roy P. The Lincoln Legend: A Study in Changing Conceptions. New York: Octagon Books, 1969, p. 108

2. Rosen, R. (1965, September). The myths by which we live. Rotarian, p. 55.

About the Author

TIMOTHY C. SMITH has pastored Blessing Heights Church in Arkansas City for more than eighteen years. He grew up a preacher's kid and spent much of his time under the training and teaching of deliverance ministries. Saved at the early age of seven in his Dad's revival in La Junta, CO, Timothy C. Smith has served as a pastor, evangelist, teacher, and even a presbyter for the Church of God of the Apostolic Faith, Inc.

Pastor Smith has two adult children. His daughter Angel lives in Arkansas City, KS with her husband John, and their two children, Jaimen and Dezi. His Son, Clay, currently lives in Tulsa, Ok and attends Victory Bible College. Diana, Pastor Smith's wife of more than twenty seven years, is the founder of Blessings Academy School.

As a preacher's kid and a pastor preaching for more than twenty nine years, Timothy

C. Smith has seen and experienced tremendous change in the spiritual atmosphere surrounding the body of Christ in America. His heart's desire is to see the church operate with the authority God has purposed in His Word.

Tim C. Smith can be reached at http://www.blessingheights.org

Made in the USA
Lexington, KY
01 March 2014